Love Letters to My Husband

Blessed Gianna Beretta Molla

Love Letters to My Husband

Edited by Elio Guerriero

With a Foreword by
Cardinal Carlo Maria Martini

Pauline
BOOKS & MEDIA
Boston

Library of Congress Cataloging-in-Publication Data

Beretta Molla, Gianna, 1922–1962
 [Tuo grande amore mi aiuterà a essere forte. English]
 Love letters to my husband / Gianna Beretta Molla ; edited by Elio Guerriero.
    p. cm.
  ISBN 0-8198-4493-4 (pbk.)
  1. Beretta Molla, Gianna, 1922–1962—Correspondence. 2. Christian saints—Italy—Correspondence. 3. Molla, Pietro, 1912—Correspondence. I. Guerriero, Elio. II. Title.
  BX4700.B42 A4 2002
  282'.092—dc21
                                        2002001919

Cover photo of Gianna and Pietro Molla in Stockholm, 1961 courtesy of the Society of St. Paul, Milan, Italy

Original Italian edition: *Il tuo grande amore mi aiuterà a essere forte Lettere al marito*

Translated by Ann Brown

Copyright © 1999, *Edizioni San Paolo,* Piazza Soncino 5, 20092 Cinisello Balsamo, Milan, Italy

All rights reserved. No part of this book may be reproduced or transmitted in any form or by any means, electronic or mechanical, including photocopying, recording or by any information storage and retrieval system without permission in writing from the publisher.

Copyright © 2002, Daughters of St. Paul

Printed and published in the U.S.A. by Pauline Books & Media, 50 Saint Pauls Avenue, Boston, MA 02130-3491.

Pauline Books & Media is the publishing house of the Daughters of St. Paul, an international congregation of women religious serving the Church with the communications media.

www.pauline.org

1 2 3 4 5 6 7 8 9   10 09 08 07 06 05 04 03 02

Contents

Foreword vii

Preface xiii

Introduction

*A Brief Biography of Blessed
Gianna Beretta Molla* 1

The Letters 17

Part I

The Engagement Letters 21

Part II

The First Years of Marriage 43

Part III

During the Trip to the United States 85

Part IV

The Last Letters 147

Conclusion 159

Foreword

"Communication," first between an engaged man and woman and then between husband and wife—that is, "communication within the family"—is both the sign and nourishment of great love, and an expression of authentic family life. Such communication, in fact, is rooted in the reality of "family," for which the engagement is an important and irreplaceable preparation, and is founded on and nourished by love. Beginning in matrimony, family life is made up of daily experiences and life-giving communication in that it is a community of persons who have "the mission to guard, reveal, and communicate love, and this is a living reflection of and a real sharing in God's love for humanity and the love of Christ the Lord for the Church his bride" (*Familiaris Consortio,* n. 17). The family, therefore, can and must be seen and defined as the first and privileged place, the origin of "communication." By its very nature and vocation, the family *is* communication— a kind of communication tending toward a total reciprocal gift of self between the spouses who feel called to live a life of two as one. In this special communication, the gift of self becomes so concrete that it brings the family closer to God the Creator and interprets his plan of love in generating and fostering new life (cf. *Gaudium et Spes,* n. 50). This makes the family the first and best atmosphere in which, day after day, the meaning of life is expressed, communicated, and developed through the educational mission of the parents.

Love Letters to My Husband, by Gianna Beretta Molla, is a simple and extraordinary example of this profound communication. "Simple" because it reveals the everyday, concrete example of Gianna and Pietro's relationship as it passed through the enthusiastic phase of passion and infatuation, when they speak the typical language of new love that engaged couples and newlyweds use; then, as their devotion deepens, their words to one another take on more profound tones of tenderness, concern, and spiritual unity. The letters reveal joy and love, and betray moments of apprehension at any sign of sickness in the children or each other. They are attentive to all the little everyday necessities (a shopping list, a list of things to take on vacation); they care for each other's problems and, in some way, share them in an attempt to help lighten or resolve them.

The letters' testimony is "extraordinary" because of the frequency, which is all the more amazing today, when communication by letter has become so rare. Their frequency shows, more than any words can, how Gianna and Pietro could not live, could not think of each other, without communicating, without revealing themselves, their feelings, what they were doing, their own joys, fatigues, worries, and their faith.

Aside from the frequency, Gianna and Pietro's written rapport is an extraordinary example of communication. It permits us a few luminous glimpses into a "life lived according to the Gospel," into that "spirituality" which characterized Gianna's experiences and those of her husband Pietro, whose letters (judging from a few comments in his wife's letters), could contribute to a more complete picture of the spirituality of this couple, this Christian family.

These letters reinforce the belief that married life is both a grace and a vocation, finding in the Sacrament of Matrimony the foundation and the paradigm of the whole experience of the couple and of the family, expressed through a life of faith and service to others.

So it was for Gianna, who witnessed to the Gospel as a wife and mother, and made Jesus her point of reference in her conjugal life. Gianna viewed matrimony and the family as an authentic and holy vocation, desiring to make of her family a "little cenacle where Jesus will reign over all our affections, desires, and actions."

She lived her married and family life with joy and complete self-giving. From the time of her engagement, she was always careful to do the will of God, in the conviction that "love must be total, full, complete, regulated by the law of God, and must last forever in heaven," and that to marry meant "to receive the sacrament of love [so that] we become collaborators with God in creation; this way we can give him children who will love and serve him."

Gianna was completely oriented toward making her new existence a total sharing with the life of her husband, truly loving him, as she desired and sought his happiness: "you know that I want to see and to know that you are happy; tell me what I should be and what I should do to make you so";

"I so want to be a joy and a comfort to you, but I sometimes wonder whether I am a burden to you." She asked pardon for every failing and for the help of correction when she had not been able to love right to the depths: "This means you have to pull my ears whenever I fail in this respect!" "Pietro, if you see me doing something wrong, tell me, okay? I will always be grateful to you if you do this."

The feeling of faith is ever-present throughout these pages in the continual reference to her own prayer, to that of her husband, and of her children: "In only twenty days, I'll be…Gianna Molla! What would you say about our triduum to prepare for our marriage? We could go to Mass on the twenty-first, twenty-second, and twenty-third, you at Ponte Nuovo, I at the shrine of the Assumption"; "…how many prayers for your family! You always find time to listen and follow the Mass. Unfortunately I can never get out…"; "Gigetto [Pierluigi] has been waiting for you since yesterday, when Zita arrived. He called to you from the window for a good fifteen minutes. To console him, I took him down the road as far as the Blessed Mother statue; there we said a 'Hail Mary' for his papa and then returned home…"

Through motherhood, she made an authentic act of love and service to humankind: "The Lord has blessed our love again, giving us another child; I am happy, and with the help of our heavenly Mother and with you close to me, you who are so good, so understanding, and affectionate, I will no longer be frightened by the sufferings of this new pregnancy."

There are also many hints of her profound Christian realism, which helped her handle trials and sufferings: "It's true, there will be sorrows too, but if we always love each other as much as we do now, with the help of God, we will know how to bear them together"; "Dear Pietro, I would never have imagined how much one suffers becoming a mother!"

These are only a few points which strike one in reading Gianna's letters to her husband. The letters are a precious testimony to conjugal and familial spirituality as an authentic journey of holiness: a spirituality—as the Church's "Directory of Pastoral Care of the Family" in Italy says—"founded on the Sacrament of Matrimony and continually nourished and strengthened by the Eucharist," which "becomes actual and is expressed not outside the conjugal and familial life, but within it, through the everyday realities and tasks which characterize it, in the fidelity to all of the demands of conjugal and family love and in their joyous actualization" (n. 112).

I offer my sincere gratitude to those who worked on this edition and, most of all, to those who, like the engineer Mr. Pietro Molla, guarded these missives with loving care, offering them now to anyone who wishes to read them. My hope is that reading these communications will prove useful to many engaged and married couples, so that they, too, following Gianna's example and helped by her intercession, may make of their time of engagement and their married and family life a "life according to the Gospel," an indestructible source of meaning and joy.

Cardinal Carlo Maria Martini
ARCHBISHOP OF MILAN

Preface

The letters that Gianna wrote to me during our engagement were bearers of enthusiasm and joy, of tenderness and love, stirring and providential invitations to enjoy the beauty of life and the wonders of creation, to live my faith with joy and trust in God.

In her first letter (February 21, 1955), Gianna went straight to the heart of my ideal when she declared, "I really want to make you happy and to be what you want me to be: good, understanding, and ready for the sacrifices which life require..."; and, "I intend to give myself to you to form a truly Christian family...."

In her later letters, her continual references to her trust in God's help and blessings and our duty to be grateful to him, confirmed to me how deeply rooted her faith was and how profound her spirit of prayer. With her invitation to celebrate our official engagement with a Holy Mass and Communion and, above all, with the suggestion to prepare ourselves to receive the sacrament of love with a triduum of Masses, Gianna edified and encouraged me.

Later in that year of our engagement, Gianna, in her humility, wrote to me: "...Pietro, if I could only be for you the strong woman of the Scriptures. Instead, I feel weak..."

In reality, she was a strong woman from the beginning. She willingly moved to a little villa on the property of the company of which I was the manager. Even during the prolonged and very worrisome strikes from 1956–1958, she did not ask to move, but rather shared in my worries and trials, supporting me in my work, knowing that living there made it easier for me to fulfill my tasks and responsibilities.

In our communion of life and love, made fuller and enriched by the births of our children, Gianna always felt fulfilled and blessed. Her letters confirm this, and I like to remember her that way.

Now, I kneel before her, a marvelous and strong woman, fiancée, wife, and mother, who, in her love for life and for the child in her womb, knew how to scale the heights of the greatest love which Jesus showed us.

Pietro Molla

❧ INTRODUCTION ❧

A Brief Biography of Blessed Gianna Beretta Molla

Gianna's Parents

Gianna Beretta grew up in a well-off and devoted Catholic family in the Lombardy region of Italy. Her parents, Alberto Beretta (1881–1942), and Maria de Micheli (1887–1942), believed firmly in remaining humble and sharing their material wealth with the needy. Alberto was an administrator in the Cantoni cotton factory in Milan; Maria had a certificate to teach nursery school, but stayed at home to care for and educate her children.

Alberto and Maria married on October 2, 1908, and moved to a house on the Piazza Risorgimento in Milan. They were often seen in the nearby Capuchin church on Monforte Street, and both were members of the Third Order Franciscans. It was from the "Poor Man of Assisi" that they derived the ideals of poverty and serenity that they instilled in their children.[1] One of their sons, Father Giuseppe, left a beautiful testimony to his parents' faith:

> Mamma was truly the strong woman of whom Scripture speaks. Her day began early, at 5:00 A.M., when Papa got up to go to Mass to begin his day before the Lord. He went

---

  1. *For this and other details, I am indebted to Antonio Rimoldi's book,* Gianna Beretta Molla, A Life for Life *(1922–1962), manuscripts.*

alone, because Mamma stayed home to prepare his breakfast and pack his lunch. After Papa left for work, Mamma passed through our rooms and woke us up, gently caressing our faces with her hand. We knew that she would leave for Mass soon, and we got dressed in a hurry, happy to be able to kneel next to her to receive Jesus in Holy Communion and give thanks with her. What wonderful words she suggested we say to Jesus! Then we returned home, had breakfast, and left for school.

Papa was a man of few words, but those few were the fruit of wise reflection. He would come home from Milan in the evening, and two or three of us would go to meet him at the station where the cable car from the upper part of town came in, to carry his lunch box and wipe any sign of tiredness from his face with our chattering. He only had to come into the house, see Mamma's smile, and hear the happy welcome of all his children to recover his serenity.

At supper, we all happily sat down at that long table after saying grace. How beautiful it is to be part of a big family! Papa liked to hear how things had gone for everyone at school, but when he heard about some trouble, his face became stern and he let us know, in a few words, that it better not happen again. While Papa smoked his cigar after supper, our oldest sister Amalia played the beautiful melodies of Chopin, Bach, and Beethoven on the piano. Finally, another important moment in our daily family life was the recitation of the Holy Rosary. Papa stood before the image of the Madonna with the older children around him, and we little ones gathered around Mamma, who helped us to respond until we fell asleep on her lap.[2]

---

2. *Testimony of Giuseppe Beretta in* Terra Ambrosiana, *1 (1994), pp. 33–34.*

Papa Alberto and Mamma Maria had thirteen children in all, five of whom died during childhood. The others were Amalia, nicknamed Iucci; Francesco, nicknamed Cecco; Ferdinando, nicknamed Nando; Enrico (the future Father Alberto); Zita; Giuseppe (future diocesan priest); Gianna; and Virginia, a future Canossian religious.

Both of Gianna's parents died in 1942, leaving behind the memory of a Christian life, lived totally and generously in the service of God and neighbor.[3]

Gianna's Childhood and Youth

Gianna Beretta was the twelfth child, the seventh of those who lived beyond childhood. She was born on October 4, 1922, the feast of St. Francis of Assisi, in her paternal grandparents' home in Magenta. In honor of St. Francis, her parents named her Giovanna Francesca. She was baptized a week later in the parish church of St. Martin by her paternal uncle, Father Giuseppe. Gianna spent the first years of her life at the house in the Piazza Risorgimento, surrounded by the love of her brothers and sisters, already breathing the profoundly Christian atmosphere of her family.

In 1925, the family moved to Bergamo, where Gianna received her First Communion on April 4, 1928, at the age of five and a half. From that day on she accompanied her mother to Mass every morning. The same year, she started school at the Beltrame di Colle Aperto Elementary School in Bergamo. She was not a brilliant student, but her family sustained her and encouraged her to study diligently.

---

3. Posizione on the virtues of Blessed Gianna Beretta Molla, manuscripts (Rome: 1989), p. 515.

In 1930, Gianna was confirmed at Bergamo's cathedral, and attended the school run by the French Daughters of Wisdom. For the final two years of elementary school, however, along with Giuseppe and Virginia, Gianna attended the school run by the Canossian Mothers, since it was closer to home and their mother was often sick. She began middle school at the public Paolo Sarti School in 1933, and it is from these years of middle school that we have Gianna's first writings. These affectionate letters written to her siblings and parents reveal how much effort it cost her to study. During the summer of 1936, she had to stay in Bergamo, while her family went on vacation in Viggiona, because she had failed the Italian and Latin portions of the high school entrance exam. She wrote to her mother: "Here I am, dear Mamma; I am all alone today, and I decided to write you so I can pass a little time in your company. I went to catechism at San Vigilio and then I went to study…"[4]

Gianna passed the exam with difficulty in September, and began attending high school in the Paolo Sarpi Institute in Bergamo. The following year, the family moved to Genoa, where she continued her studies with the Dorothean Sisters in Quinto al Mare. There, in the spring of 1938, she participated in a course of spiritual exercises preached by the Jesuit, Father Michele de Avedano. These exercises were a significant influence on the life of the fifteen-year-old, and her Christian spiritual life deepened and matured during this time. In a notebook entitled "Remembrances and Prayers," she took notes on Father Avedano's sermons, wrote prayers to recite during the day, and enumerated her resolutions to live a devout life. As a result, Gianna's scholastic efforts improved so much that she was promoted with good grades at the end of the year.

---

4. *Letter of September 6, 1936.*

Gianna's health was becoming a concern, however, and her parents decided at the beginning of the following school year to keep her home to rest from the demands of studying. Gianna accepted this decision with good grace and filled her free time with a series of enjoyable activities: she practiced the piano each day, taught by her mother; she painted nature scenes, expressing her love for creation; she helped with the housework. Most important, she had more time to get to know and participate in Catholic Action, an organization in which she remained involved for many years and through which she developed her charism as a leader. Another gift of that year were her meetings with Father Mario Righetti (1882–1975), one of the protagonists of the liturgical movement in Italy, who passed on to the young girl a great love for the Church's public prayer.

After her year of rest, Gianna took up her studies again at the high school of the Dorothean Sisters in Genoa Albaro, working hard and earning consistently good grades. In 1941, the Second World War had begun. Genoa was continually being bombed and Papa Alberto's pernicious anemia had worsened, so the family decided to return to Bergamo. Gianna and Virginia stayed in Genoa to finish high school.

In April 1942, Mamma Maria died suddenly, and Papa Alberto died only a few months later in October. Gianna missed her parents deeply, but she energetically continued her studies and her dedication to the life of the Church. She obtained her diploma in June of 1942, at the height of the Second World War.

After the death of their parents, the family decided to stay in Magenta. Gianna chose to study medicine, following in the footsteps of Ferdinando and Enrico. Above all, she wanted to help her neighbor and give joy and serenity to those who suffered. Gianna attended medical school in Milan until the city became too dangerous because of the war. In 1945, at the beginning of her fourth year, she transferred to Pavia to continue her studies.

After the war and the fall of fascism, Italy began to rebuild under a republican form of government. Along with many other young Italians, Gianna became deeply involved with the renewal of her country. Focusing her energies on Catholic Action, Gianna became the delegate for the youngest girls, and was responsible for encouraging their spiritual growth and education. From 1946 to 1949, she was the president of the Young Women's Branch. Assisted by her sisters and by Sister Marianna Meregalli, a Canossian religious who became her close friend and spiritual guide, Gianna undertook many projects for the girls: conferences, pilgrimages, and outings. She often used her own money to help the neediest girls.

Many people recall Gianna's way of listening with charity, rather than lecturing, to educate the girls of Catholic Action. One of her girls declared: "In her apostolate, she looked above all to charity, to approaching everyone individually; she was interested in every interior or family problem and was always ready to help with a word of encouragement, counsel, and comfort."[5]

In addition to her work with Catholic Action, Gianna also worked to promote the Christian Democratic party in Italy, which strove for a victory in the 1948 elections. Even with her many activities and interests, however, Gianna managed to study hard. On November 30, 1949, she received her long-awaited medical diploma and opened an office in Mesero (only 5 km from Magenta), the following year. The full entry into her pro-

---

5. *Testimony of Enrica Parmigiani recorded by Fernando da Riese,* Un "sì" alla vita. *Gianna Beretta Molla (Rome: San Paolo, 1980), p. 45.*

fession made her even more dedicated to her work. She brought to her work a kind of "practical idealism," which united the science she studied with the faith she so firmly held. Her notes from that time indicate her views:

> Today there is too much superficiality in our work. We care for bodies, but many times incompetently.... We must do our part well. Study your science. We must be honest doctors, filled with faith. We must care for our patients with kindness and gentleness, remembering that these are our brothers and sisters; have delicacy and respect. Do not forget to also administer to the soul of the sick person.[6]

Gianna wanted most to care for children and mothers; in order to further her knowledge and better serve her patients, she took a specialization course in pediatrics in Milan. She also dreamed of joining her brother, Father Alberto, a missionary in Brazil who was building a hospital in Grajau with the help of their brother Francesco, an engineer. Gianna wanted particularly to help the mothers in Brazil, who lacked proper gynecological care, especially during pregnancy and birth. With this in mind, she studied Portuguese and looked into a course in obstetrics in order to prepare herself.

She wrote to her brother: "Dear Father Alberto, I'm so happy to be coming, and I really think this is my calling. I prayed about it, and at the end of the month I'm going to make a retreat to see if the Lord will tell me 'yes' or 'no.'"[7]

When Francesco returned to Italy and told of the many hardships and illnesses that flourished in the tropical climate of Brazil, the family grew fearful. They knew that Gianna, very

---

6. *This text, classified as Document 27–31, is recorded in* A. Rimoldi, *cit., p. 131.*
7. *Letter to her brother, Father Alberto, dated September 1952.*

much like her mother, could not tolerate hot weather, and they advised her to change her mind. Her spiritual director and the bishop of Bergamo agreed with her brothers and sisters. Bishop Bernareggi said: "From my experience as a priest and bishop, I have learned that when the Lord calls a worker into his vineyard, he prepares that worker for the task and provides for everything. I don't know whether this is your sister's authentic vocation. So many obstacles stand in the way...."[8] Gianna listened to their words and was particularly moved at the mention of her mother; in her youth, Maria had wanted to go to the missions, but she had become an extraordinary mother instead. Despite the disappointment of the moment, Gianna turned from her dream of becoming a missionary and focused her attention on her "mission" at home.

Engagement and Marriage

Toward the end of 1952, realizing she was not meant to go to the missions, Gianna passed through a time of uncertainty about her vocation. By the end of 1954, however, a new path began to unfold before the young doctor. She had, on occasion, met an engineer, Pietro Molla, in her office and in her parish. As vice-president of La Saffa, Pietro Molla was leading the match and plastics factory toward great expansion. On December 8, 1954, they met formally at the first Mass of Father Lino Garavaglia, future bishop of Cesena. There, Pietro, 42 years old, and Gianna, 32 years old, discovered a mutual attraction. It seemed as if a veil had suddenly been removed and each discovered the beauty of the other, the common ideals of love of fam-

---

8. *The text is recorded by her brother Giuseppe Beretta in* Terra Ambrosiana, *1 (1994), p. 36.*

ily, children, and neighbor, long cultivated and protected from inquisitive eyes. Gianna was a beautiful woman and Pietro quickly fell in love with her. She fascinated the engineer and drew him out of the solitude and excessive work that threatened to dominate his whole life. Pietro gave a sense of security to the young woman who was in search of her path in life. They started dating and soon they began to discuss engagement and marriage. In a memoir addressed to his children, Pietro wrote: "From February (1955) onward, we met more and more frequently; we confided our desires and aspirations, hopes and certainties to each other; we understood each other better and better."[9] At the end of February, Pietro proposed marriage, and Gianna joyfully accepted.

Some of the most beautiful letters in this book are from that time of their new love and engagement. Gianna and Pietro were by no means adolescents, but their letters reveal a love that was fresh, youthful, tender, and enthusiastic. Gianna wrote to Pietro, "I want to make you happy and be what you desire: kind, understanding, and ready for the sacrifices that life will require."[10] Pietro responded: "I have read your letter many times and I have kissed it. A new life is beginning for me; a life with your great affection and luminous kindness. We are beginning a life of love together."[11] They were officially engaged on April 11, when they exchanged rings and a promise of fidelity; the preparations for the wedding began right after this. Gianna spent the time of her engagement in joy and fear, cultivating sentiments of self-giving, and preparing for her life with Pietro. She often alluded to Prov-

---

9. *Recorded in* Posizione *on the virtues, p. 452.*
10. *Letter of February 21, 1955.*
11. *Letter of February 22, 1955.*

erbs 31 in her letters: "A strong woman, who will find her? The heart of her husband can trust in her. She will do only good things for him and never bring evil upon him throughout all of his life." The Bible exalts the practical, yet affectionate and faithful woman: this model constantly inspired Gianna. She prepared herself spiritually for marriage, but she also took delight in the practical preparations: choosing furniture for their future home, buying tablecloths and bedding, and having her wedding dress made.

Finally, September 24 arrived and the couple testified to their love before Christ and the Christian community. When the bride entered the Basilica of St. Martin with her brother Ferdinando, spontaneous applause broke out. Father Giuseppe, Gianna's brother, celebrated the wedding, and then the couple left on their honeymoon in southern Italy.

On their return, the newlyweds settled in Ponte Nuovo, in a house on La Saffa's property. Gianna returned to her medical work and Catholic Action. She was nominated President of the Women, a post she would hold until her death. Gianna remained close to her brothers and sisters after her marriage—she wrote to Father Alberto and Mother Virginia, far away in their missions, and she spent much time with Zita, Francesco, and Ferdinando, who lived nearby. She often had Ferdinando's daughters, Iucci and Maria Vittoria, spend the night with her when Pietro was away on business.

In the spring of 1956, Gianna realized with joy that she was pregnant. Pierluigi was born November 9, 1956, to the immense happiness of his parents. The baby boy was baptized by his uncle, Father Giuseppe, and was immediately consecrated to Our Lady of Good Counsel; this began a custom that they would follow with each of their children.

Exteriorly, the couple's life changed little: Gianna continued her medical work, and Pietro worked as hard as ever, developing new products at the factory. But the child's presence gave a new vigor to their conjugal affection and created new bonds of love. With their happiness came some challenges: Pierluigi, affectionately called "Gigetto," seemed to be growing with a dislocated hip, Gianna suffered from burning pains in her stomach, and Pietro was overwhelmed with work. Still, the little family continued to grow in love for one another.

Toward the end of the spring of 1957, Gianna again discovered she was pregnant. Gianna and Gigetto, along with some of Gianna's relatives, spent the summer in a rented house in Courmayeur. Pietro, busy at the factory, was only able to visit on the weekends. In September, the situation was reversed: Pietro stayed in the mountains with Gigetto, while Gianna returned to Magenta to care for her patients. That December, ten days after her due date, a girl named Maria Zita was born, whom everyone affectionately called "Mariolina."[12]

The beginning of 1958 was particularly difficult for the couple. In February, Pietro had to go to Sanremo for a time to rest from the pressures of his work. Gianna stayed home to care for the children; Pierluigi was afflicted with acetonuria, while Mariolina slept very little at night. Gianna accepted these difficulties in the love of Christ.

In the summer of 1958, Gianna went back to Courmayeur to vacation with her two children. Gianna described the positive

---

12. *Mariolina died at the beginning of 1964, about two years after her mother. A boarding student at "The Smile of Italy" in Imperia, directed by Sister Luigia, Pietro's sister, Mariolina contracted an eruptive disease and was transported to the hospital in Milan. Unfortunately, not even the Milanese doctors could avoid the worst, and Mariolina died a devout death while she recited the Hail Mary.*

effect of the time in the mountains on Pierluigi and Mariolina to her brother, Father Alberto: "Pierluigi and Mariolina are well. We came back from Courmayeur fifteen days ago, and the children are beautiful, have good color, and are eating well."[13]

About a year after Mariolina's birth, Gianna was again pregnant, and she relayed this news with great joy to Father Alberto, who was in Italy for the summer. Gianna wrote: "I will have the great joy of asking you to baptize my third baby, who, if all goes well, should arrive around the beginning of July. Are you happy, Uncle?"[14]

In late spring of 1959, Pietro had to take a long business trip to the United States, from April 26 to June 17. Gianna suffered greatly from his absence, which coincided with serious health problems related to her pregnancy. She had to go to the hospital in Monza on June 15 for terrible pain and spasmodic contractions, which made her fear she was losing her baby. With the prompt intervention of the doctors, she recovered and was able to go to the airport to meet Pietro on June 17. Laura Enrica Maria was born on July 15, 1959. Gianna told her friend, Mariuccia Parmigiani, the news: "Wednesday morning (July 15), at 8:15, Lauretta was born. You can't imagine how happy we are, first of all because all went well, thanks be to God; then because she is beautiful and healthy, and also because she's a girl, and I really wanted a little sister for Mariolina. I know from experience how precious sisters are, and the Lord answered my prayer."[15]

---

13. *Letter to her brother Father Alberto, dated September 24, 1958, her third wedding anniversary.*
14. *Letter to Father Alberto, December 2, 1958.*
15. *Letter to her friend Mariuccia Parmigiani, dated July 18, 1959.*

This was perhaps the most beautiful time of Gianna and Pietro's married life. A few months after Lauretta's birth, Gianna's desire to spend more time with Pietro came true when she accompanied Pietro on a business trip to England and Holland. They arrived in London on Sunday, December 11. Gianna wrote to Father Alberto: "I traveled every day, either by train or by car, to the various little towns near London, so I've been...to Norwich and Great Yarmouth, and I've been able to get an idea of these little towns, their customs, and their way of life. It only took an hour and ten minutes to fly from London to Amsterdam, a city crisscrossed everywhere by canals.... Tomorrow evening (Sunday, December 18), or Monday evening at the latest, we'll return to them [the children] and get ready for Christmas with them."[16] The couple also traveled together to Denmark and Sweden in July 1961, and Gianna saw with her beloved the places he had already told her so much about.

Urged on by love, Gianna wanted another child. According to the testimony of her brother Ferdinando, she suffered two miscarriages after her third pregnancy from undetermined causes.[17] When Gianna returned from her trip of July 1961, however, she discovered she was having another baby. During the second month of this pregnancy, a fibroma developed on the lateral right wall of the uterus, and she had to go to the hospital in Monza for treatment in September 1961. The doctors presented Gianna with three choices: an abortion, which would certainly save her life and allow her to have more children; a complete hysterectomy, which would assure her life, but preclude another pregnancy; or the removal of only the fibroma,

---

16. Letter to Father Alberto, dated December 17, 1960.
17. In Posizione *on the virtues, cit., p. 47.*

which was potentially dangerous for her and the child. As a doctor, Gianna entirely understood the risks of the third option, but she chose to put the life of her child before her own at all costs. Dr. Vitali, the surgeon at Monza hospital, removed the fibroma and Gianna was able to return home after a short stay in the hospital. She sent her children, who were on vacation in Courmayeur with her friend Mariuccia Parmigiani, a loving note from the hospital to reassure them:

> My dearest treasures, Papa is going to bring you many big kisses; I wish so much that I could come too, but I have to stay in bed because I have a little tummy ache. Be good children and do what Mariuccia and Savina tell you… I hold you all here in my heart and I am thinking about you every minute. Say a Hail Mary for me, so that Our Lady will help me get better quickly, and then I can come back to Courmayeur and hug you and stay with you always. Your Mamma kisses and hugs each of you with much affection.[18]

After the operation in September, Gianna knew that there could be grave complications with regard to the baby or to herself, but she made an effort to live in serenity. She took up her medical work again and lovingly watched over the growth and education of her children. She prayed with growing intensity that she might be spared the sacrifice of her life. She was extremely clear with Pietro and her family on one point: "This time it will be a difficult delivery, and they may have to save one or the other—I want them to save my baby."[19] Her trust in God gave her the strength to continue to hope. Only once, according

---

18. *A note attached to the letter to her friend Mariuccia Parmigiani, dated September 13, 1961.*

19. Posizione *on the virtues, cit., p. 79.*

to Zita, was she momentarily overcome with sorrow. "Finding herself alone, she called me in tears. Immediately I had our brother Francesco—who couldn't stand emotional displays—go to her, and she had enough courage to change it into something to laugh about."[20]

Gianna went to the hospital in Monza on April 20, 1962, Good Friday. The next morning, Holy Saturday, she underwent a C-section for the birth of her fourth child, Giovanna Emanuela. Just a few hours after the operation, as the anesthetic was beginning to wear off, she began to feel excruciating pain, which only increased during the following days. It was a slow agony, interrupted by sad farewells to her newborn daughter, to her family, to Pietro.[21] In a moment of lucidity, she asked to return to Ponte Nuovo to die in the house which had guarded the sacrament of her love. She died Saturday morning, April 28, 1962, after having probably heard, for the last time, the voices of her children who were just waking up in the next room.

Her Beatification

One of those who remained near Gianna during her last sufferings was an extraordinary priest who, for love of the poor, lived as a beggar in Bologna. Father Olinto Marella had built a

---

20. Ibid.

21. *Once again, from the memoir-dialogue of her husband: "I remember when you told me, on Wednesday morning, with such solemnity, that it almost seemed otherworldly: 'Pietro, I am cured now. Pietro, I was already on the other side, and if you only knew what I saw. Someday I'll tell you. But since we were too happy, too comfortable with our marvelous children, full of health and grace and all of heaven's blessings, they sent me back to suffer some more, because it is not right to present ourselves before the Lord without having suffered much.' This was and remains for me your testament of joy and suffering." From Pietro Molla—Elio Guerriero, op. cit., p. 102.*

Boys' Town using materials given to him by La Saffa; he well knew Gianna's generosity and love for her neighbor.[22] At her funeral, Father Marella was already speaking of her sanctity, and on the first anniversary of her death, he printed a booklet in which he gave public testimony to a mother who gave her life with unbounded generosity, and acknowledged the veneration of the faithful for her, in the hope that the hierarchy would recognize her:

> …Whenever her name is repeated, her example will live on like that of a saint. If obedience to the canonical prescriptions does not permit such a title to be used in the sacred liturgy until the highest authority in the Church has thus decided and consented, one can certainly pray and invite others to pray with this [example] of maternal love.[23]

The priest's invitation was promptly welcomed by the ecclesiastical authorities. The bishop of Milan at the time, Cardinal Montini, who would shortly become Pope Paul VI, took an interest in Gianna's case. Bishop Carlo Colombo, who was very close to Cardinal Montini, was one of the promoters of the cause for beatification. The process was begun in 1972 with the gathering of testimonies and the expansion of the critical biography by Antonio Rimoldi. Based on this material, Pope John Paul II gave the *nihil obstat* for the introduction of the cause in 1980. The diocesan process was concluded in 1986 with the authorization of Cardinal Carlo Maria Martini. The decree of heroic

---

22. *Regarding Father Olinto Marella, whose cause for beatification has been officially opened, cf.* L. Bedeschi, Padre Marella: Un prete accattone a Bologna *(Cinisello Balsmo: San Paolo, 1998).*

23. Gianna Beretta Molla, *booklet printed by the Graphics School of Father Marella's Boys' Town, Bologna, 1963.*

virtues was issued in 1991, a miracle was recognized in 1992, and on April 24, 1994, John Paul II solemnly proclaimed Gianna a blessed. On that occasion, Cardinal Martini declared: "The example of Gianna Beretta Molla, in addition to that of other mothers of yesterday and today, is a sign of hope and an incentive to families and to all of us."[24] Gianna's beatification, therefore, is a recognition of all mothers and all Christians who have pursued and are pursuing the way of sanctity in the family.

The Letters

The publication of Blessed Gianna Beretta Molla's love letters to her husband represent a renewed and significant chapter in Christian spirituality. These letters are a convincing demonstration that the way of sanctity can unfold not only in the religious life, but also in the midst of the world, by living one's vocation as a spouse and parent. This ancient Christian truth about vocation became almost buried along the centuries of Christendom. Among the diverse types of saints—martyrs, confessors, doctors, virgins—there did not seem to be a conspicuous place for those who had embraced marriage and family as their God-given mission. Those few saints who were married, such as Rita, Nicholas von Flue, Frances of Rome, Jane de Chantal, and Louise de Marillac, had, in a way, renounced matrimony. Gianna Beretta Molla, on the other hand, is a witness to the joy of a life of communion with another individual. In her letters, we see the strength and tenderness of her love for her husband and children. In Gianna's life, it is clear that her love for

---

24. *John Paul II—Carlo Maria Martini,* Gianna Beretta Molla: Una santa della quotidianitá, *Milan: Centro Ambrosiano, 1994), p. 82.*

Christ intensified and deepened her love, attraction, and passion for her beloved, and strengthened her instinct and will to dedicate herself to her children.

Gianna unified her love for her family with love for her Savior, creating the foundation of her life and final sacrifice. Today, this Christian concept of matrimony is often misunderstood and neglected. The example of the devoted Christian life that is presented in Blessed Gianna Molla is powerful in its demonstration of the beauty and sanctity of the family. The exchange of love between spouses that is reflective of the love of Christ for his Church reveals the grace of married life, the grace that brings spouses to salvation, that infuses holiness in their children, and spreads God's love to those around them. The working of this grace and the holiness that can be attained in marriage and family is the essential element in the beatification of Gianna Beretta Molla, and is what we see manifested in her letters to her husband.

In the first part of the aforementioned biography, Antonio Rimoldi painstakingly lists the writings, documents, and testimonies concerning Gianna. The second chapter, in particular, lists the letters, notes, and postcards written by Gianna Beretta Molla to her husband, her family, and her friends, as well as various acquaintances. Rimoldi counted 157 writings, from July 15, 1936 (a postscript Gianna wrote in a card her mother was sending to her brother in the military service), to March 1962 (a note written to Mother Emma Ciserani, a Canossian nursery school teacher in Magenta), about a month before her death.

The seventy-three letters to her husband contained in this book cover the period from February 1955 to February 1961. To help the reader, the missives have been divided chronologically, into four sections: letters from the time of her engagement, the first years of marriage, the time of [her husband's] business trip to the United States, and her last letters.

Gianna's life spanned a time when the world underwent great changes: from the development of fascism in Italy, to World War II, to the technological and political developments that followed the war. There is an echo of some of these changes in her letters. Pietro's position at La Saffa, for instance, was on the cutting edge of emerging industrial technology; in fact, Pietro introduced the use of the recently developed formica in the laminates plant that he managed, and contributed to the development of increasingly used electrical appliances. Television was also just becoming accessible, and Gianna mentions some of the popular shows on the RAI television network in Italy at the time. Pierluigi also enjoyed listening to popular Italian music, which, as in America, was gaining a wider audience among young people. Gianna died on the eve of the Second Vatican Council, but the changes that would be spurred on by that Council began before Pope John XXIII was elected. As a member of Catholic Action, Gianna took an active role in the Catholic lay movement in Italy with its social and political aims.

Gianna was certainly a "woman of her time," but she was also a timeless woman in her love for her family and for God, in her complete dedication to life, not only the lives of her children, but the lives of her patients and everyone around her. Yet, through these letters, we can see not only the saint, but the woman struggling with pain, sadness, worry; the wife and mother striving for happiness, love, comfort for herself and her family. A simple narrative of her life would reveal only half of Gianna's story. Only with her own words can the story of her sanctity and her humanity be complete.

❖ PART I ❖

The Engagement Letters

FEBRUARY 1955–SEPTEMBER 1955

The eleven letters that Gianna wrote to Pietro before and during their engagement reveal her enthusiasm and her happiness at having discovered her vocation. Filled with a combination of energetic joy in living and a peaceful reflectiveness, her character and personality are unfolded for the reader. For Gianna, falling in love with Pietro began the fulfillment of what she had been teaching her girls in Catholic Action for so many years. She had said in a conference on October 21, 1946:

> To be called to family life does not mean getting engaged at the age of fourteen.... Now is the time to begin to prepare yourself for family life. You cannot follow this path if you do not know how to love. To love means to want to perfect yourself and your beloved, to overcome your egoism, and give yourself completely.

Gianna had lived these words since her adolescence, acquiring throughout her life the principles which formed her: from her family she learned the joy of life, love for poverty, simplicity, and acceptance of the will of God; in Catholic Action she became convinced of the mission of the laity to be a presence and witness in the world; in her work as a doctor she put into practice these truths and saw the reality of God's love manifested in her patients. Thus, by the mid-1950s, Gianna reached the culmination of her formation and she was prepared to give herself completely in love to her future husband.

The engagement letters are an introduction to Blessed Gianna Beretta Molla and her developing relationship with her future husband. Through them, we see a vibrant young woman who found joy in nature and children, who cherished every moment of life, and who was falling deeply in love. In each letter, it is clear that Gianna was growing closer to Pietro and was striving for a spiritual union with him in preparation for the Sacrament of Marriage. It is this union which is most striking about these letters, illustrating a harmony between the physical and the spiritual, between the person and God as the couple came to know and to do God's will in love for one another.

1

Gianna and Pietro attended a ballet together on New Year's Eve at La Scala in Milan, and they started dating at the beginning of 1955. In the conversation to which Gianna refers in the following letter, the couple had spoken of engagement and the possibility of forming a family together.

Gianna also refers to a time of sadness in her life, when her parents died just a few months apart in the same year.

FEBRUARY 21, 1955
Monday

Dearest Pietro,

I hope you don't mind if I begin this letter by calling you by your first name and using such familiar language. After sharing our thoughts so openly yesterday, I think we can assume this level of intimacy, which will help us to understand and love each other more and more.

I want to make you happy and be what you desire: kind, understanding, and ready for the sacrifices that life will require. I haven't told you yet that I have always been very sensitive and eager for affection. While I had my parents, their love was enough for me. Then, although remaining very united to the Lord and working for him, I felt the need for a mother, and I found her in the dear nun whom I told you about yesterday.[1]

---

[1]. Sister Marianna Meregalli knew Gianna in Magenta from 1945–1949. She was very close to Gianna in the years of her personal search following her parents' death and her apostolate in Catholic Action.

Now you are here whom I love, and I intend to give myself to you, to form a truly Christian family.

Ciao, dear Pietro. Pardon my familiarity, but that's how I am.
With affection,
Gianna

2

In 1955, Pietro Molla, an engineer, was the director of La Saffa, a large factory on the outskirts of Milan. His primary job was to plan new products, and his workload was often heavy—he certainly did not lack "work and worry."

MARCH 11, 1955

Dearest Pietro,

I don't know how to thank you for all your thoughtfulness and kindness. Thank you for the beautiful roses and for the hours we spent together last night. You know, I feel bad because I'm stealing your precious hours of sleep, when you need to rest after a day of work and worry. On the other hand, I am so happy in your company that I wish time would stand still when I'm with you.

Pietro, if only I could tell you all I feel for you! But I can't—you will have to read between the lines. The Lord has truly blessed me. You are the man I had wished for, but I often ask myself, "Will I be worthy of him?" Yes, worthy of you, Pietro, because I want so much to make you happy, but I fear not being able to do so, and I often feel I am unable to do anything. When this happens, I ask God, "Lord, you see my desire and my good will. Supply what is lacking and help me to become the wife and mother you desire and which I think Pietro wants, too." Is that all right, Pietro?

I greet you with so, so much love, your

Gianna

3

Since her childhood Gianna had spent many vacations in the mountains. She loved the outdoors and had a genuine appreciation for nature, especially for the alpine hills where she loved to ski.

> Sestriére
> MARCH 21, 1955
> *Monday evening*

Dearest Pietro,

Now I feel happier because I heard your voice on the phone. As I told you, it snowed all day today, but I skied for about four hours anyway. To make up for the cloudy day, all the stars are out this evening, so I hope tomorrow will be nice. I am really enjoying the wonderful atmosphere and service of the hotel—the only thing missing is you, Pietro. I'm already looking forward to the joy of having you with me this weekend. I will pick you up so that I can spend the last hours of my vacation with you. Thank you for the beautiful outing in Switzerland on Saturday. You're too good to me—I don't deserve it at all, but I promise to do all I can for you in return.

Do you still have a lot of work to do? It doesn't seem fair that you're there working, while I am here doing nothing. If only I could send you a little bit of this fresh air, I would do it with all my heart!

Ciao, dear Pietro, give your dear parents my greetings, and *arrivederci* with much love, your

Gianna

❧ 4 ❧

Gianna always loved going to daily Mass and she continued to do so during her vacation. In the following letter, the spiritual union that was forming between the two young people is clear, as they prepared themselves for their engagement.

Sestriére
MARCH 23, 1955

Dearest Pietro,

I found your letter today at lunchtime when I came back from skiing. You can imagine how happy you made me with all of your sweet and affectionate expressions of love. Thank you, dear Pietro, I love you too, very much, and I know we will always love each other. You're so good and intelligent that you'll always understand me and we won't be able to disagree. I'm sorry you were so busy with work on Monday. My thoughts are always with you, and if I could help you I would do it with all my heart.

Yesterday and today we had beautiful, sunny weather. I get up at 8:00 in the morning (what a lazybones! you are already in the office!) and go to Mass at 8:30. I have never enjoyed Mass and Holy Communion as much as I do here. The beautiful little church is always quiet and empty. The celebrant doesn't even have an altar boy, so I have the Lord all to myself, and all for you, Pietro, because already, where I am, you are too.

After breakfast, we leave right away with our skis and down the trails we go! I usually go skiing with the instructor for a little while around 11:00 A.M., and—all modesty aside—I have learned to ski even some difficult slopes. But don't worry—wherever it's too steep, the instructor has us go down the easier way. It's marvelous on the mountain, though. When you're up high with the blue sky and the white snow, how can one help but rejoice and praise God!

Pietro, you know how happy I am when I'm surrounded by nature; I could spend hours contemplating the beauty of creation.

Around 3:00, after lunch, a brief nap, and a little walk, I go back to the slopes until about 6:00. After that, the time drags; I'm lucky to have Piera[1] here—she's so much fun and we laugh so much!

So that is how my days go—a little bit different from yours, poor Pietro, always working.

Two more days and then we will see each other, what joy!

Gianna

---

1. Pierina Fontana was a co-worker and friend of Gianna's from Catholic Action. The two women were planning to get married on the same day, but an obstacle arose which prevented this.

❧ 5 ❧

The self-giving love that was growing between the couple, seen in this letter, continued to bear fruit throughout their life together. Pietro said of Gianna, "From the beginning, and in almost every letter, she returned to this request: 'Tell me what I should do to make you happy.' It was not difficult for me to respond to her love. If her goal was to make me happy, what could I do but strive to make her happy?"

>Sestriére
>MARCH 25, 1955
>*Friday*

Dearest Pietro,

I'm sending you some pictures of me, and I hope you will like them. The weather is always beautiful here—we are very sunburned!...

You won't recognize me when you see me, my face is so burned—here red, there black, a little of every color. Creams are useless. Our attraction to the ski slopes is so strong that we ignore our burned faces and go back anyway.

My dear Pietro, my happiness would be complete if you were here with me to enjoy this fresh air, but we will spend our next vacation together, right?

I want to be a joy and comfort to you because you deserve it and need it with all your work. This means you have to pull my ears whenever I fail in this respect!

Ciao, dearest Pietro. Waiting to embrace you again tomorrow, I send you the most affectionate greetings.

>Your
>*Gianna*

❧ 6 ❧

Gianna and Pietro's official engagement was set for April 11, but Pietro gave Gianna the engagement ring a few days earlier.

April 9, 1955

My dearest Pietro,

How can I thank you for the magnificent ring? Pietro dear, in exchange, I give you my heart and I will always love you as I love you now. You are the dearest person to me, and my thoughts, affections, and desires are continually turning toward you on this eve of our engagement. I can't wait for the moment when I can be yours forever. Pietro dearest, you know that I want to see and to know that you are happy; tell me what I should be and what I should do to make you so. I have great trust in the Lord, and I am certain that he will help me to become your worthy spouse.

I often meditate on the text [associated with] St. Anne: "A strong woman, who will find her? The heart of her husband can trust in her. She will do only good things for him and never bring evil upon him throughout all of his life."[1]

Pietro, I want to be that strong woman for you! Instead, I feel weak. This means that I must lean on your strong arm. I feel so safe, so close to you! I ask you a favor: from now on, Pietro, if you see me doing something wrong, tell me, okay? I will always be grateful to you if you do this.

---

1. *This is the beginning of the famous passage praising the virtuous woman, found in Proverbs 31:10–31.*

With much love, I embrace you, and I wish you a blessed Easter.

Your

Gianna

The letter that Pietro sent in reply to this one is significant and touching in its illustration of their profound love for one another:

> My dearest Gianna…you are the strong woman I asked of heaven, and our heavenly Mother answered my prayer. I will always trust my whole heart to you and I will receive everything good from you.
>
> Love me always as you do now; always be affectionate and good, thoughtful and sweet and understanding as you are now. This is how you are already making me happy and how I ask you to make me happy always.
>
> To me you are the strong woman of the Gospel.

7

Like most engaged couples, Gianna and Pietro experienced some challenging moments during their engagement, as the following letter indicates. Pietro's parents, Luigi Molla (1884–1956), and Maria Salmoiraghi (1885–1978), were very attached to their son. This attachment gave rise to a slight misunderstanding which caused Gianna some concern.

April 18, 1955

My dearest Pietro,

Today of all days, when I wasn't expecting to enjoy your dear company, I have you even closer to me: I received your letter. Pietro, thank you for being so good and affectionate. Your words touched me, and I'm happy that in answer to my question, "How should I be to make you happy?" you answer I should continue to be good, affectionate, and understanding as I am now. I will, dearest Pietro, and it will be easy, because you are so good to me.

I already knew that you loved me, but being reminded of your love through your letter today filled my heart with joy. Just think, Pietro, what a great gift the Lord has given to us—how thankful we must always be for it!

Pietro, I promised you that I would always tell you my worries. I must tell you about something which causes me to suffer.

I'm afraid your parents aren't satisfied with me, that I am not what they wanted for you. I know you always have been and still are the center of their affections, and now I feel like I'm taking you away from them. And while I love them because they're your dear parents, I don't feel for them the affection I think I should because they have always shown me such delicacy and kindness.

If I made you sad by telling you this, forgive me.

Ciao, dear Pietro, be happy, and many big kisses from your

Gianna

❧ 8 ❧

In this next letter, the source of Gianna's concern about Pietro's parents is revealed, as is Gianna's firm resolve to make her future husband happy.

JUNE 10, 1955

My dearest Pietro,

Knowing that it gives you so much pleasure to receive my scribbles, I am sending you these few lines to tell you again how happy I am....

Dear Pietro, last Sunday when your mother said that if she should ever see you unhappy, she wouldn't know what to do, I began to wonder if perhaps I'm not the right person for you, that I'm not good or understanding enough. Now, though, after your repeated reassuring words, I am at peace and rejoice to know that you are happy.

Dearest Pietro, I don't know how to thank you for the beautiful doctor's office you're preparing for me with so much love.[1] When it's finished and I move in, I will have you even closer to me in my work; in this way, you, too, will alleviate suffering and give joy to my dear patients.

I love you so much, Pietro, and you are always with me, starting in the morning during Holy Mass. At the Offertory, I offer your work, your joys, and your sufferings along with mine; then I repeat the offering all day long until evening.

---

1. Gianna is speaking of the doctor's office that Pietro was preparing close to his parents' home. This would be a more spacious and cheerful office than the one Gianna was renting in a house in Mesero.

I wish I could see you every day, but…that would be too greedy of me. When you're tired, you must tell me and not beat around the bush, so I'll send you home earlier—do you understand? You're already tired from work, and I wouldn't want to be a cause of your falling apart.

Ciao, take care of yourself, and many kisses, your
Gianna

9

July 1, 1955
Tuesday evening

My dearest Pietro,

It's 9:00, the time when my dear Pietro generally arrives. But not tonight—it's Tuesday! You'll tell me I'm too greedy and that I exaggerate, but the more time I spend with you, the longer I want to be you; the more I know you, the more I love you. Dear Pietro, that's life. And I will write to you tonight so that I can visit with you a little.

Pietro, thank you for your love for me; I wanted a good, kind man, and the Lord has placed one by my side. I so want to be a joy and a comfort to you, but I sometimes wonder whether I am a burden to you. You're so often tired, but affectionate, and I always keep you with me for hours!

While we were choosing furniture on Sunday, I could already feel the warmth of our little house, all beautiful, new, and shining. Thank you for your perfect understanding and efforts to fulfill my desires.

Think, Pietro, about our nest, warmed by our love, and joyful with all the little *popi*[1] the Lord will send us! There will be sorrows, too, of course, but if we always love each other as we do now, then with God's help, we'll know how to bear them together. Don't you think so?

For now, though, let's enjoy the happiness of loving each other. I was always told that the secret of happiness lay in living

---

1. *"Popi" is a term for "babies" in the Lombard dialect. Gianna used this expression often to show her affection.*

one moment at a time and in thanking the Lord for everything he sends us. So, let's lift up our hearts and be happy!

Ciao, dearest Pietro. I'm not expecting an answer; I wrote only to pass the evening with you and to tell you how much I love you.

Big kisses from your
Gianna

10

Gianna continually revealed to Pietro her piety and her deep faith and invited him to share in her spiritual journey. Pietro recalls this habit of hers with fondness and respect: "she invited me to participate in liturgy and piety, while at the same time proposing to me a new model of humanity."[1] Gianna always had a strong concept of human communion in prayer, especially with her beloved Pietro.

September 4, 1955
Saturday evening

Dearest Pietro,

I was waiting for you and was beginning to think something had happened to you, but your phone call relieved my fears. My Pietro, you know how happy I am when I can see you and be with you, and when anything prevents us from being together—even though the reasons are just—my heart…protests, though my mind says "It's right, this is the right thing to do." Tonight, then, I'm writing to you in order to chase the blues away.

Pietro dearest, I want you to feel me very close to you these days, because you can't imagine how much I miss you when you are so far away. You'll say I'm exaggerating, but it's true. You are my Pietro, and I am already one with you in heart and soul.

You are so good, dearest; you love me so much, and I love you very, very much. Your joys are mine, and all that worries you or makes you sad worries me and makes me sad, too.

When I think of our great, beautiful love, I can do nothing but thank the Lord. It's true that love is the most beautiful gift

---

1. P. Molla—E. Guerriero, op. cit., p. 46.

that God has given to us. And we'll always love each other as we do now, Pietro. In only twenty days, I'll be…Gianna Molla! What would you say about our making a triduum to prepare for our marriage? We could go to Mass on the twenty-first, twenty-second, and twenty-third, you at Ponte Nuovo, I at the shrine of the Assumption. The Blessed Mother will unite our prayers and, because strength is found in unity, Jesus can't help but listen to us and answer our prayers.

I'm sure you will say yes, and I thank you.

Just think, the next time you travel, I will be there, right beside you, telling you over and over—until you're tired of it—that you are my whole life.

A thousand thanks, Pietro, for the magnificent little house you have prepared for me. I couldn't have wished for anything more beautiful. Soon it will be my turn to give to you by making it always warm and cozy.

Buon viaggio, dearest Pietro, and…don't miss the train next Sunday!

Many, many kisses from your
Gianna

❖ 11 ❖

On September 10, Pietro wrote to his soon-to-be wife: "Gianna, I want to be the husband of your fondest dreams and your most holy and joyous desires, a husband worthy of your virtues, of your goodness, and of your immense love."

September 13, 1955

My dearest Pietro,

I can't find the words to thank you for the wonderful and loving letters that you have sent so faithfully these past few days. Every letter, every expression gave me so much joy. You are a treasure, Pietro, and the more I read your letters, the more I know that you are so good and you have within you many virtues hidden by your humility, but seen and appreciated by your Gianna.

Thank you for everything, Pietro. I want to tell you all that I feel, all that is in my heart, but I can't. But you already know what my feelings are, so you must know how to understand me.

Dearest Pietro, I'm sure that you will always make me as happy as I am now and that the Lord will listen to your prayers, since they come from a heart that has always loved him and served him in a saintly way.

Pietro, how much I have to learn from you! You are such a fine example for me, and I thank you for it. With God's help and blessing, we will do all we can to make our new family a little cenacle[1] where Jesus will reign over all our affections, desires, and actions.

---

1. *The couple particularly liked this expression, and it became an image to which they often referred.*

My Pietro, our wedding is just a few days away now, and I feel very moved to be so near receiving the sacrament of love. We will be working with God in his creation; in this way we can give him children who will love and serve him.

Pietro, will I be able to be the wife and mother [of your children] you have always wanted? I hope so, because you deserve it and I love you so much.

> I kiss you and embrace you
> with all my heart, your
> *Gianna*

❖ PART II ❖

The First Years of Marriage

DECEMBER 1955–JULY 1958

There are twenty-four of these letters, most of them written during their first two years of marriage while Pietro was away on business trips. In this time, their first two children were born: Pierluigi and Maria Zita (Mariolina).

These letters show the deepening of Gianna's love for Pietro and her affection for her children. During these years, the passion and love that the couple had for one another matured, but did not diminish. The birth of their children strengthened the bond between them as they rejoiced in bringing forth new life and dedicated themselves to their growing family.

❦ 1 ❧

After only a few months of marriage, Pietro had to travel to Switzerland for business. Gianna stayed home and spent much time with her family, including Ferdinando's two daughters, Iucci (Amalia) and Maria Vittoria, who came to stay with her in Pietro's absence.

December 14, 1955
Tuesday afternoon

My dearest Pietro,

You have been gone now for a whole night and half a day, but I'm thinking of you every moment and you are always present to me. When I got home from Magenta last night, I stopped by your parents' house to reassure them and say hello to them again for you. Then after I had supper with my family, Zita came back to our house with me.

Pietro, you'll say I'm exaggerating, but the house is so empty and sad when you are not here! I started to write Christmas cards while I waited for the nightly news, but my Pietro did not appear on the show. I said the rosary, prayed for our family, and with my dear treasure in my heart and mind, I went to sleep.

I was planning to get up for the 6:00 A.M. Mass, but guess what woke me up instead? The beautiful sound of your phone call! So I went to Mass in Magenta with Zita at 8:30 A.M. Then I picked up Iucci and returned to Ponte Nuovo with Zita.

Iucci was all excited, as she brought her pajamas with her. She will stay for a day and then it will be Maria Vittoria's turn. As you can tell, I have plenty of company. You, on the other hand, have to travel all alone in that cold Switzerland. Dress warmly, Pietro, and don't get too tired. I wish I could help you in your work, but I can't do anything except pray that God will always protect and help you.

My Pietro, I'm very happy because I love you, and you love me too, and I will always do everything I can to be a good, affectionate, understanding, and smiling little wife.

A big, big kiss, and an
affectionate hug from your
Gianna

2

DECEMBER 15, 1955
Wednesday evening

My dearest Pietro,

You're traveling as I write—I wish I could be with you to help pass the hours on the train!

Today was a dreary day, rainy and foggy; it was dark outside, and a little dark in my heart, too, knowing you're so far away. But time will pass, and soon it will be Tuesday…and we'll take up our life again, the beautiful hours of intimacy and affection that I wish would never end. How are you? Is it very cold there? I think of you so often, Pietro, and now that you are so far away, I realize more than ever how much I love you and how I can't live without you. I went to Mass this morning in our little church and I prayed to our beautiful Mother for you, Pietro, that she would help and protect you.

Mariuccia[1] came at noon and wanted me to go to lunch with her and Zita in Bernate, and I had to go to please her.

After lunch I went to the Crespi farm on a call, and then I went to Mesero. I explained your itinerary to Papa and Mamma again, and eased their worry by telling them that you would be staying in a hotel tonight.

Pietro, I would like to write to you every day, but I'm afraid you might not get my letters. I think of you all the time, and I can't wait to hold you again.

---

1. *Mariuccia (Maria Bambina Parmigiani), was a close friend of Gianna's from 1942 until her death.*

Take care of yourself, and don't get too tired. With much love, I kiss and embrace you.

Your
Gianna

Zita sends her love.

❧ 3 ❧

This note marks the first anniversary of Gianna and Pietro's engagement; Pietro had been in Paris and was on the train returning home.

APRIL 11, 1955...
APRIL 11, 1956

My dearest Pietro,

One year has passed since the day we were engaged: a year of intimate joys, understanding, and great love.

The most beautiful thing I can wish for you with all my heart is this: many, many years like this one, and may the Lord always bless and preserve our great love.

I kiss you with all my affection,

Gianna

❦ 4 ❧

In April 1957, Gianna was pregnant with her second child, Mariolina, who would be born on December 11, 1957. Pierluigi, born on November 19, 1956, was only about five months old at the time. This was a difficult pregnancy, during which Gianna's faith in God and the Blessed Mother, and her love for Pietro sustained her. The joy and quick smile that were familiar to everyone who knew her were often the result of her willpower, rather than her feelings.

APRIL 1957
Thursday evening

My dearest Pietro,

How could I fail to respond to your beautiful letter? Dear Pietro, what a great comfort your love is to me!

The Lord has blessed our love once more by giving us another child—I am happy, and with the help of our heavenly Mother, and with you close to me, you who are so good and understanding and affectionate, the sufferings of this new pregnancy no longer frighten me.

Thank you, dearest Pietro, for your prayers. The Blessed Mother will surely listen to us, and we will have another beautiful child like our little Pierluigi. What a dear little angel he is! Every day he is more lively—he seems to understand when we talk to him.... Isn't it a consolation, Pietro? Every time I kiss him when you're away, I kiss him for you, too. Who knows how often you must think of him when you're away and wish he were near you! I'm so glad there are only four days left until you come back; I'm already looking forward to the joy of seeing you again, of embracing you, of finally seeing you with some free time to spend with your little angel. How sweet you always look when you have your little boy in your arms and you make him smile! And when he reaches out his little arms to caress you, what a beautiful picture you make! When he lisps his first words, he will be even more precious. Now he speaks with his little blue eyes, always smiling and waving his arms and legs.

And now, Pietro, I have a great favor to ask of you. Please forgive me when I am in a bad mood or depressed; I try to be cheerful, but I don't always succeed. I hope it's just a result of these first months [of pregnancy]. Your great love will help me to be strong and conquer myself.

I am waiting for you, Pietro, with all my love.

I kiss you and embrace you, along with our dear little angel,

Your most affectionate
Gianna

❧ 5 ❧

The family spent their summer at a vacation house in Courmayeur; Pietro's vacation did not start until July 28, but Gianna and the baby went ahead and waited for him.

In this letter, Gianna sent her mother-in-law special greetings; there had been some misunderstanding between them, which Gianna wanted to heal with her affection.

July 15, 1957

Dearest Pietro,

I just got home from the travel agency with the coupons for 30 liters of gas, which I am sending to you right away in the hopes that they'll arrive on Saturday. They'll give me the rest after July 25.

It's 5:30 P.M. now and Pierluigi has been sleeping peacefully for almost two hours—if only he would always sleep that way!

It's a bit chilly outside today. The sun comes out for a little while and then disappears. I took Pierluigi for a walk in the woods with Adelaide[1] and the children for about an hour. He had such a good time, the little angel! I hope you're feeling better. Take care of yourself and don't overdo it, understand, my dear Pedrin?

When you come, please bring me my rosary. Thank you. Give Mamma my love and thank her for all she does for us and for you while we're away.

---

1. Adelaide Agnese Molla was Pietro's sister.

I'll be expecting you early Saturday morning, you can imagine how eagerly! It's too bad we will only have two days…but the 28th will come soon!

>Many, many big kisses from your Pierluigi and from your most affectionate
>
>*Gianna*

⋆ 6 ⋆

In this letter, Gianna tells Pietro of her daily concerns for their son, Pierluigi, who had to wear a brace because of a dislocated hip.

JULY 16, 1957

My dearest Pietro,

It's only 8:30 P.M., but we have already finished supper. Our treasure has just fallen asleep, after a little bit of fussing while trying to get comfortable. You are, however, unfortunately still in Milan. Pietro dear, it would be too beautiful if we could be together all of the time; everything seems more beautiful when you are with me, and all my worries over Pierluigi decrease with you by my side. Patience! Let's offer it to the Lord so he will help our dear little one bear his first suffering and get perfectly well. I promised a daily rosary to the Madonna of Guérison[1] for him. What I wouldn't do to keep him from suffering! He did manage to sleep a few hours today with his brace on, though.

Let's hope for the best.

Ciao, my dearest Pietro, and good night,

your
Gianna

---

1. This is a little shrine near Courmayeur, where Gianna often went to pray.

7

This note was sent with the previous letter.

JULY 17, 1957
Wednesday morning

Pietro dearest,

Before sending this out, I wanted to let you know how Pierluigi is doing. He slept with his brace on last night, and he woke up every hour, but without crying or fussing. He always went right back to sleep in my arms with his little smile. I gave him his bottle at 6:00 A.M., and he drank it all; then I took his brace off, and he wriggled happily until 8:00 A.M. He's asleep now.

I can't wait to hear your voice on the phone today.

But for now, many, many big kisses from your dear Pierluigi and your

Gianna

Many special greetings to your Mamma.

❖ 8 ❖

Gianna loved going high in the mountains, and she often took her children to the top of Checrouit, the hill above Courmayeur.

July 18, 1957
Thursday evening

My dearest Pietro,

Yesterday, I got your express letter from Monday, and today I received the one from Tuesday. My Pietro, you really are a treasure. You know how much I love your letters and how much comfort they bring me, so you never fail to write to me. Thank you so much.

Our dear little angel is getting used to his brace; he puts up with it very well during the day (we try to distract him as much as possible), and he doesn't cry very much at night, even though he wakes up every few hours to turn over. He has a good appetite now, and a rosy little face, just like a little shepherd. And all this is because of his dear Papa, who chose an enchanting little place with lots of sunshine from morning till night for us to have our vacation. I love to think that in fifteen days, you will be here with us to rest and enjoy this wonderful fresh air.

We all went on a picnic yesterday from 1:30 to 3:00 in a beautiful spot, only about 15 minutes from the house; Pierluigi loved it! He came home in a very good mood, and even though he can't talk yet, he shows how happy he is by wriggling and squirming in his brace. Then he slept well for a couple of hours. We went to church at 6:30 to say the rosary, and when we got home, he ate his cereal and fruit with a great appetite. His day ended at 8:30. I gave him a big kiss from his Papa and then, off to sleep!

Today, we spent the day at Checrouit. When we got up this morning, there was marvelous sunshine and a clear, bright sky, and it was not at all cold. We packed up the bags and took the cableway up—Flavio and Giancarlo[1] were very excited. Pierluigi was very lively, and everyone in the car smiled at his cries of joy.

At the top of the mountain, I put his brace on and he slept for about an hour. Then, since it was getting a little bit windy, we went down to the meadows, where Pierluigi drank his bottle with great appetite. You'll see what a tanned little face he has on Saturday.

I found your second express letter when we got home. What a dear husband and saintly Papa our children have! Even though your work keeps you busy, you always find time to think of us and pray for your dear family! I can never thank the Lord enough for giving me a companion as dear, good, and affectionate as my Pietro.

I hope your pain is gone and that your toothache doesn't keep you from eating and resting.

I'm sorry I forgot to give you the little bottles of medicine. But I think resting in the peace of Courmayeur will do you the most good.

Thank Mamma for her affectionate greetings and please give her mine and Pierluigi's. Tell her I'm very tranquil because I'm sure no one can ease the separation from your family like she can.

Ciao, Pietro dearest, many, many affectionate kisses from your Pierluigi and from your most loving

Gianna

---

1. *Flavio and Giancarlo were Pietro's nephews.*

❧ 9 ☙

In September, the situation of the couple was reversed: Pietro was in Courmayeur with the baby, while Gianna had to return to work in Mesero. Gianna stayed with Francesco and Zita in Magenta while Pietro was away.

SEPTEMBER 17, 1957
Tuesday morning

My dearest Pietro,

Before I go to Ponte Nuovo to air out our beautiful house, I'm sending many, many kisses to you and to our dear little angel who will be ten months old on Thursday! I'm glad Gigetto's cold is almost gone. I kissed him before I left yesterday morning and even though he was asleep, he smiled; seeing that smile, I felt a little less sad at having to leave.

I wish we could always be together, but unfortunately... I have a lot of patients right now—I'm in the office a good two hours every day. Tonsillitis, bronchitis: the Asian fever has probably reached Mesero. But it's nothing serious; it's gone in two days.

The weather here is beautiful, though it's a bit chilly in the morning and evening. I hope it's nice at Courmayeur, too, because good weather makes people happy and is good for their health. In any case, if it gets too cold, let me know and I'll come pick you both up right away.

I'll call Sister Luigia[1] tonight before 6:00, so I can tell you what she says. Rosetta[2] is starting her vacation, which will last until the end of the month. Adelaide is tired of volunteering for work and stayed home yesterday. I told her to relax, that a little rest wouldn't hurt even her. Flavio is always riding his bike on the new paths and zooms around like a madman, as usual.

I'm glad those gentlemen came to visit you yesterday. Visits from good people are always a pleasure. If Mr. Marzola[3] should come, let me know ahead of time so I can bring everything we need for lunch.

Ciao, dear Pedrin, many big kisses to my Gigetto and to you, and affectionate greetings to Mamma and Savina,[4]

from your
Gianna

---

1. Sister Luigia Pagani was a Canossian sister who worked with Gianna from 1942 to 1947.

2. Maria Rosa Ramazzotti occasionally worked in the Molla home.

3. Ivo Giovanni Marzola, an engineer, was the manager of the glue factory located on property owned by La Saffa.

4. Savina Passeri worked for the Mollas from 1956 to 1962.

10

September 20, 1957
Friday afternoon

Dearest Pietro,

When I got back from Mesero, Rosetta told me you had called. I was so disappointed not to hear your voice and Gigetto's. You had just missed me; it's better if you call me between 6:00 and 6:30 P.M.—that way I'll be sure to receive the phone call myself.

Anyway, thank you for letting me know everything is fine. How hard it is to be away from you! My thoughts are always with both of you: I imagine you, all loving with our treasure, and our dearest Pierluigi filling the house with his shrieks of joy.

How beautiful he is! Everyone who sees him admires him. Thanks be to God that he's so healthy and is such a lively and sweet baby.

Your faith, dearest Pietro, gives me hope for a complete healing of his stiff neck. I must admit that I worry a lot about that problem. May the dear "Notre Dame de la Guérison" hear our prayers!

They are broadcasting the *Manon Lascaut* of Puccini from Spoleto as I write to you—that music is always so beautiful and touching!

Zita and Cecco left for Bergamo at 7:00 A.M. Cecco had to pick up a tool that he had left in Brazil from a man who has just returned from there. I decided to stay home because I was afraid I would get too tired. I sent the film to Bergamo, though, and asked them to develop it as soon as possible.

And so I'm all alone with you, dearest Pietro. Try to stay well, darling, and promise me that you'll take better care of your health. Medicine helps, yes, but what counts the most—you know it very well—is rest. Think of Gigetto and the little one that we're expecting so eagerly, of your Gianna who loves you so much, and who wants to see you healthy and always happy.

Don't worry about me; I try not to tire myself, partly because my feet are starting to swell. I go over to the house every day to clean up a little and give the plants some light and air. Zita takes good care of me and is happy to have me here with her.

Mother Virginia comes almost every day, too, because Nando is teaching her how to do x-rays. She is hoping the Reverend Mother Provincial will buy an x-ray machine.

It's 11:00 A.M., so I'll stop my rambling. Please excuse my bad handwriting.

Big, big kisses to my Gigetto, special greetings to Mamma and Savina, and a big hug to you from your

Gianna

11

Gianna and Pietro's second wedding anniversary was on September 24. Though they were not together on their anniversary, Gianna looked forward to being reunited with Pietro and Pierluigi when she and Zita picked them up in Courmayeur.

SEPTEMBER 25, 1957

My dearest Pietro,

Your magnificent flowers and your sweet words were very touching. Infinite thanks to you, to my Gigetto, and above all to the Lord who loves us so much.

I'm enclosing the note from Father Agostino[1] so you can reply as you see fit.

Zita will be happy to come on Saturday, and we should be there around 5:30 P.M., if we leave here around 2:30 P.M.

I'm so happy you're both coming back because…having you close is [so much better than only writing letters].

Many greetings to Mamma and Savina.

Big kisses to my Gigetto and to his dearest Papa,

your most affectionate
Gianna

---

1. *Father Agostino Cerri was the archbishop's delegate to Ponte Nuovo di Magenta and later the parish priest.*

❧ 12 ❧

On Sunday, February 16, Pietro left for Sanremo to rest from the excessive pressures of his work. Gianna remained at home with the children: Pierluigi at the time was about two years old, Mariolina had been born on December 11, 1957 and was just over two months old.

Pietro spent time during this vacation with his sister, Sister Luigia, a religious in the Congregation of the Most Precious Blood. Sister Luigia was the director of the school called "The Smile of Italy" in Imperia.

February 18, 1958
Tuesday

Dearest Pietro,

I was happy to hear last night on the phone that everything is fine. I hope the weather stays nice so that you can stay outside in the sunshine as much as possible. Here, it's cold and snowy, so Pierluigi can't go outside. He's venting his energy by playing records and dancing. He seems to be feeling better, as I told you—he didn't throw up at all yesterday. Unfortunately, he did earlier today, but his color is back and he looks more rested; let's hope he's just feeling sick because he's teething. But he has been sick now for ten days, and he should be better by now. Dear Pietro, I could never have imagined how much I would suffer being a mother! I always want to see our children beautiful and healthy, without having to suffer, but instead, there is a little thorn in our happiness every day…. It's a good thing you're more optimistic than I am, so you can encourage me—otherwise, my morale would be almost below zero.

As I write, I have Mariolina here beside me, looking at me with her beautiful big eyes and smiling every time I say her name. She cried a little bit last night; I don't know why. Fortunately, Zita was here to take care of her. I wish I could comfort her myself during the night, but it is still impossible for now—the two of them are still too little and they would disturb each other too much.

Does it bother you that Zita is coming to help me a little while longer? I ask you this, Pietro dear, because I sometimes feel like you're not happy about it.[1]

I keep thinking how happy Sister Luigia must have been to have you with her for almost a whole day. When you see her again, give her many, many greetings from me.

Many big, big kisses from your dear little angels.

Stay well and happy, rest and eat. Understand, Pedrin dear? With all my love I embrace and kiss you,

your most affectionate

Gianna

Many big kisses, Papa, from your Pierluigi.[2]

---

1. On the letter are the words "on the contrary," written by Pietro the first time he read the letter.

2. This sentence was written at the "request" of Pierluigi.

13

FEBRUARY 19, 1958
Wednesday afternoon

Dearest Pietro,

A little note today too, and a big, big kiss from your "popi" and from your Gianna. Both Pierluigi and Mariolina had a good night last night. Gigetto ate a big lunch today with good appetite and didn't throw up. Let's hope he continues that way. Mariolina spits up a little and is a bit cranky, but she is asleep for now. Whenever he sees your hat, Pierluigi says "Ma…ma…" which for him means "Papa." Zita says that in the evening he goes to the hall and pounds on the storm door with his little hand, calling "Mamma" and "Ma"! What a treasure! He tries to express all his thoughts with these two little words.

It snowed yesterday afternoon, but today is clear and beautiful, though there's a strong wind.

Pierluigi has been invited to his cousins' house in Magenta on Friday.[1] I haven't been able to get to Milan yet, so I'll have to buy him a hat and mask [for Mardi Gras] in Magenta.

I saw your Mamma, and she told me to say hello for her and tell you to rest because you need it.

I would like to bring Pierluigi with me when I come to pick you up. What do you think? Will it be too tiring for him? Many, many big kisses from the little ones and from your

Gianna

Are you all right? And your teeth?
Greetings from Zita, Cecco, and Savina

---

1. *She is referring to Ferdinando's daughters, Amalia and Maria Vittoria.*

14

Pietro's absence was a challenging time for Gianna, as the children were having some small health problems, and she longed to have her husband by her side. She strove to be patient, waiting for his return...

February 20, 1958
Thursday evening

My dearest Pietro,

I hope you're still doing well. Today I received—or rather, we received—your cards. Thank you, and many big kisses from your little ones.

Mariolina cried non-stop yesterday afternoon, and didn't quiet down until 2:00 A.M. She was vomiting a lot, so I had Mr. Crotti take us to Milan to see Dr. Cislaghi[1] today. Nando came with us, and since Mariolina had to go, I brought Gigetto along as well.

Unfortunately, nothing can be done for Mariolina; we just have to wait until she can eat cereal, when she's about five months old. The doctor gave me some drops to relieve her stomach pains, but said there's nothing to worry about: she looks healthy and rosy, not a bit pale, and he said that whenever she cries a lot, we can use some suppositories to calm her.

In Gigetto's case, though, the doctor found him well and strong, the vomiting is due to hyperesthesia, so any little irritation (from a cough, a bread crumb, etc.) will cause vomiting. This will pass, too, as he gets older.

---

1. Mr. Crotti was the Mollas' chauffeur; Dr. Cislaghi was a well-known pediatrician.

Now I feel better, and with the help of God and all my good will, I'll try to be patient and wait for them to get older! I brought Pierluigi over to your Mamma's this morning, since I had to go to Cuggiono to see one of my patients in the hospital. She was delighted to take care of him for me; she said he didn't cry, but he pouted and refused to talk. As soon as I got back, though, he started jumping and playing as usual. Today he wanted to eat and he didn't throw up. He went to nursery school, but he didn't like the [Mardi Gras] masks—he was a little afraid of them.

We are always thinking about you and can't wait till we can give you a big hug again. Try to stay well, dear Pedrin, and "catch" the many big kisses from your little angels and your

Gianna

Greetings from Zita and Cecco

❧ 15 ❧

Februdary 22, 1958
Saturday afternoon

My dearest Pietro,

The 1:00 P.M. siren [signaling the end of lunchtime at the factory] just sounded, and while the little ones take their nap, I will take advantage of this time to send you our love.

I hope you're all right, and that your "I'm okay" last night on the phone wasn't hiding anything. I've been thinking of you visiting with Sister Luigia—how sad she'll be not to see you so often after your vacation! But everything comes to an end—both the good things and the bad.

Pierluigi was very rambunctious during lunch and didn't want to eat; halfway through, he threw up. What a shame, Pietro dear! I loved watching him eat two or three little bowls of cereal. Now I never know what to give him…patience! It will pass, as the doctor says. Mariolina is doing well today—she slept through the night and hasn't cried.

There's a ball at the Nuovo Hotel in Magenta today for "Fat Saturday." Mr. Molla and his wife were invited, too. It begins with refreshments at noon, and the ball will take place in the evening. I'm glad to hear you went to the concert—time will pass more quickly for you if you go out. Only one more week, dear Pietro, and then we'll be together again.

Nothing new is happening [at the factory], Adelaide says, so don't worry and just stay healthy.

Hello from all of us and big kisses from your little ones.

With all my love I embrace you, your

Gianna

❦ 16 ❧

Gianna often seemed uncertain whether to share her worries about the children with Pietro; in his absence she bore the burden of their little problems, but expressed concern over whether she should tell him of her difficulties.

FEBRUARY 23, 1958

Dearest Pietro,

Finally, I have a moment of peace. Mariolina is having a bad day today—after two days of quiet, she cried a lot today, but now she's asleep. Gigetto wants to go outside in the garden all day to play with the little stones. Just think how much fun he'll have at the beach! Your Mamma is here visiting Adelaide and helping me, since Rosetta is on vacation this week.

It's 10:00 P.M. now, so I'll start over. I was happy to hear your voice on the phone, to know you're doing well and that your spirits are high. I'm sorry Pierluigi didn't say "Mamma" or "Ma." The poor little thing had just finished throwing up. It's a good thing he likes milk and doesn't throw it up, otherwise I don't know how he'd survive.

Mariolina has settled down a bit. I gave her some chamomile tea and that seemed to calm her.

Pietro, please forgive me if I cause you pain by telling you these things, but you are my Pietro, the Papa, and telling you about things helps to lessen my worries.

You were right to switch hotels. Besides, you're closer to Sister Luigia now.

I'm sorry I won't be able to come and pick you up; I'll do it next time.

Ciao, Pedrin, one more week and then you'll be home.

Big kisses from Gigetto, little smiles from Mariolina, and a most affectionate embrace from your
Gianna

17

February 26, 1958

My dearest Pietro,

Pierluigi and Mariolina are asleep. I'm listening to "Everyone's Songs" on TV as I write. Tagliavini[1] is singing "You will come back to me," etc., you know, from the "Potato." You will have to tell me later why it is titled the "potato." My dearest Pedrin, I'm sorry your days of rest are already over, but I'm glad I'll be able to embrace you again in a few days. Every night, whenever the doorbell rings, Pierluigi rushes to the door, hoping to see his "paparino." Every time, he shakes his head and comes back into the hall protesting. When he saw me leaving the house this morning to go to the nursery school, he started to cry so loudly that I couldn't bear to leave him home.

So he came along with me. At first, he played with the other children and the toys, but then he began to call for me, so they brought him to my office. When he saw me in my doctor's coat, he was frightened and began to cry. He did get used to seeing me dressed that way, though, and when the children who came to see me cried, tears welled up in his eyes, too. My little doctor!

Today he seems to be feeling better; he only threw up a little bit this evening, but he looks pale and isn't hungry.

Mamma was here for supper, and she was hoping to talk to you, but she didn't realize I was planning to call you tomorrow evening instead. She is well and says hello. She constantly speaks to Pierluigi about you, and Gigetto answers by shaking his little head "no," as if to say you're not here.

---

1. *Renzo Tagliavini was a popular singer at the time.*

I ran in to Father Luigi[2] in Magenta today and he asked if you were home. He wanted to stop by and tell you that Monsignor's eightieth birthday is on Tuesday March 9,[3] and he would like you and Nando to serve Mass at 6:00 P.M. Nando called and asked me whether you would accept. I thought you would—will you? Anyway, you can talk with him when you come back.

Ciao, my dearest husband, stay happy.

> Beautiful big kisses from your
> three treasures, your
>
> *Gianna*

---

2. *Father Luigi Gallozzi was the assistant pastor in Magenta from 1931 to 1967.*
3. *Monsignor Luigi Crespi was prevost of Magenta; his birthday was on March 3.*

· 18 ·

Before leaving on summer vacation, Gianna left a note for Pietro, who was in England on a business trip. At six months old, Mariolina seems to have had a dislocated hip, just like Pierluigi had, and required a brace.

Magenta
SUMMER 1958

Dearest Pietro,

Macciocchi (the orthopedist) said everything is okay. However, given her weight, he recommends that Mariolina wear the brace at night for two more months. Thanks be to God!

Ciao, dearest Pedrin, don't get too tired. I'll call you Monday night at 7:30.

Big kisses,
Gianna

❧ 19 ❧

July 6, 1958[1]
Sunday evening

My dearest Pietro,

I'm glad to hear everything went well, and I'm eagerly waiting for you to arrive here. Gigetto has been waiting for you since yesterday, when Zita arrived. He called to you from the window for a good fifteen minutes. To console him, I took him down the road as far as the Blessed Mother statue, where we said a "Hail Mary" for his Papa and then returned home, hoping that Zita would come in time for supper. She and Mamma didn't arrive until midnight, though.

I'm sending you the thermos with Zita because it fell and broke. I bought it in a shop on the corner of Orefici Street and Cordusio; they told me they would replace the glass inside if it ever broke. It would be good if you could buy another thermos, even a small one, with a wide mouth, for Gigetto's risotto—it's so hard to get it out of narrow ones.

Then don't forget your clothes: overcoat, umbrella, shoes.

I'm also sending you the coupons for gas,[2] and buon viaggio!

Many big kisses from your beautiful and precious little ones. Everyone admires them and compliments us for them.

A most affectionate embrace and I hope to see you soon,

your

Gianna

---

1. The date of this letter was reconstructed by Monsignor Rimoldi, since Gianna only indicates the day of the week (Sunday). There is, however, some uncertainty as to whether it was actually Sunday the sixth or Sunday the thirteenth. The dates of the successive letters are reconstructed from the supposed date of this one.

2. The Val d'Aosta area offered its residents gas coupons in Gianna's time.

20

JULY 9, 1958
Wednesday

Dearest Pietro,

We're all fine here. The babies are already tanned and are eating well. Mariolina is making me a little desperate, though, because she doesn't want to wear the brace anymore. I had to take it off last night so she would go to sleep; let's hope she won't have to wear it much longer.

I took them to the pine woods above Villais yesterday. Mariolina wriggled her legs in the sun, happy to be free of the brace for a while. Pierluigi spent his time energetically throwing little stones in the ditch. Poor Gigetto, he calls you fifty times a day, and every time he hears a car, he says "Mamma…Papa," then shakes his head and says "Grandma," since he thinks you have gone to Grandma's in Magenta.

The record player isn't working today. Tell Menescardi he's a fine trickster and have him give you another one. Pierluigi loves his music, and if it starts to rain, we won't be able to settle him down without it.

We forgot the white centerpiece for the 45 rpm records.[1]

I'm waiting for the booklet [of gas coupons] for the Fiat 1100; I'm sending you fifteen of the twenty-five liters that I've gotten, since I already used the other ten. Remind Cecco to let me have his car's log book.

I haven't seen Mrs. Valle [the landlady] yet.

---

1. *The centerpiece was used to change 33 rpm records to 45 rpm.*

How come Nando hasn't arrived yet? Are the children sick?

Don't worry about the white polish for Pierluigi's shoes; I found some here at Courmayeur. The weather is mixed today: some sun, some rain, some wind. Fortunately, the children haven't caught anything—not even a sneeze.

Try to take care of yourself, dear Pietro, and don't work after supper—rest. Remember what happened last year?

Looking forward to hearing your voice tonight, I greet you and kiss you with all my affection along with our beautiful little ones,

Gianna

Greetings to Mamma

· 21 ·

The Mollas always welcomed their family and friends into their home. Vacations were often a special time for Gianna to spend not only with her husband and children, but also with her brothers and sisters. Father Giuseppe, a priest in the Bergamo diocese, visited his sister along with his friend, Father Piero, who is mentioned in the following letter.

July 14, 1958
Monday evening

Dearest Pietro,

I'm sending you the gas coupons now so that they'll arrive in time for you to use them. I hope you had a good trip and that you won't feel too much of a difference in temperature when you get to Ponte Nuovo. We finally had some sunshine this afternoon. Father Giuse and Father Piero went up to the Turin lookout to enjoy the sun and the gorgeous view while I took the little ones for a short walk. As usual, Pierluigi greeted each car that passed with a hopeful "Papa." I put him in your bed this morning to make him feel better, so he wouldn't miss his "paparino" quite so much.

Mrs. Valle stopped in to ask what we're planning to do next year. I told her I had to talk to you about it before giving her an answer. Someone asked to rent the house year-round, but she prefers to give it to us because we only rent it for a couple of months in the summer. I really don't know what to tell her: if we intend to come to Courmayeur again next year, it would be best to stay here, since it's so nice and all the rents are about the same around here. Come to think of it, fifteen days at the beach are enough—any longer and the children would just get cranky and overtired. What do you think?

Ciao, my dearest Pedrin, we'll be together Friday evening.
Big kisses from your little ones and from your
Gianna

22

July 16, 1958
Wednesday afternoon

My dearest Pietro,

There have been thunderstorms since this morning. Pierluigi is asleep now, and Mariolina is here chattering to me, mamma…pa…pa—she gets more mischievous every day! When she's not wearing her brace, she likes to sit and play on the swing or the little chair.

I went to Morgex[1] with Gigetto and Gianfranco to get some meat—I also bought some for Laura and Mr. Furlan[2]; then I bought a laminated blue-and-white checked tablecloth at the market so the white tablecloths won't have to be washed so often. Pierluigi was very pleased to be able to walk in the rain with his umbrella. Laura's children are feeling better; the fever is gone, but they're full of little scabs.[3] They have to be quarantined for fifteen more days before they can go out.

Gronchi[4] is arriving on Saturday; everyone was going crazy on the phone Monday. They hired four extra phone operators, two for daytime, two for nighttime at the Royal, where they had to put in a direct line to Rome. There were officials at the Stipel who had to talk to Rome and Turin, so we poor unimportant beings had to wait over an hour to place a call.

---

1. A tourist town about 10 km south of Courmayeur.

2. Luigi Furlan was the owner of a textile factory in Mesero.

3. Laura Viola was Ferdinando's wife; their children had been sick with some sort of exanthematic illness.

4. Giovanni Gronchi was president of the Italian Republic from 1955–1962.

Amalia de Zoverallo[5] wrote to me and said the Sisters tried the Saffa "Lily" soap and liked it so much that they want to buy it in bulk. Does it still cost sixty lire if they buy a lot of it at once? I'll write to Amalia and then give the order to Adelaide.

I'm sorry it's so hot in Rome and that you have to stay in the city. When you come back from Rome you should come up here for a few days to rest before leaving for Spain. Can you?

Ciao, say hello to Mamma for me; many kisses from your little ones, from Gigetto, who calls you, shakes his head, and then blows you a kiss.

A hug from your
Gianna

---

5. *Amalia Zoverallo, Gianna's unmarried cousin, was also her godmother and Confirmation sponsor.*

23

July 20, 1958
Sunday evening

My dearest Pietro,

It's about 10:30 P.M. and our beautiful little ones are sleeping tranquilly after enjoying the sunshine almost all day long. I say "almost" because it rained for a little while this afternoon. It's calm and clear now, though, and I can see the beautiful starry heavens. Adelaide, Cecco, and Zita left half an hour ago, happy after spending a lovely day with their beloved nephew and niece. I'm thinking of you traveling right now, your heart here with us. Dear Pietro, it would be so wonderful to be able to be together, united, all of the time. Luckily, your vacation begins in only ten days: what joy!

Pierluigi misses you very much. How often he calls for you! How affectionate he is! When you're not here, he won't leave me for a moment: "Mamma…Mamma…." Maybe he's afraid I'll leave him like I did on Friday. How beautiful they are! Mrs. Valle was here for a while the other day and compared her three-year-old girl, who is much smaller and thinner than Pierluigi, to them. We must always be so grateful to the Lord for giving us two great treasures who are beautiful, healthy, and robust. Mariolina is even doing better now—thanks be to God! I go to church every morning to thank God for all the graces he is continually giving us, and to ask him to help me be a good mother and to make you happy every moment.

I'm including a list of things for you to bring when you come, and also Gigetto and Mariolina's sizes [for clothing].

Take care of yourself, my Pietro. I wish you buon viaggio in Spain: enjoy your trip and don't feel sad about being far away from us.

> Many big kisses from your three treasures, your
> *Gianna*

24

July 21, 1958
Monday evening

My dearest Pietro,

Today was a gorgeous, sunny day. As I already told you [on the phone], I took everyone to Checrouit. Pierluigi held his breath until the cable car started moving, then he began chattering—you can imagine how the other passengers watched and complimented him. When we went in the chair lift, he observed everything from up high: the fields, the flowers, the cows, and he liked it so much that he didn't want to get off at the end!

Mariolina didn't cry at all. I made her some cereal on the little camp stove, while Gianfranco "took care" of the fire. All in all, we had a wonderful day, completed by your telephone call. Did you hear how loudly Gigetto called you, and what big kisses he sent you!

I thought you had already gone to Barcelona by plane. If it tires you less and you get there faster, it would certainly be better [than the train].

I'll be waiting for your telegram and, above all, we'll be waiting for you with open arms on Tuesday the twenty-ninth. Tell Mr. Lazzari[1] that the doctor has ordered you to take another month of complete rest. If you don't take it now, when will you rest? Remember to bring the calcium injections (in the kitchen cabinet).

Ciao, dear Pietro, buon viaggio.

---

1. *Mr. Lazzari was the general director of La Saffa and Pietro's immediate superior.*

Big kisses and hugs from your dear little ones and from your

Gianna

Greetings to Mamma
Gianfranco wants me to remind you to bring him the stamps.

❧ PART III ❧

During the Trip to the United States

APRIL 1959–JUNE 1959

Pietro had to take a long business trip to the United States from April 26 to June 17, 1959; during these fifty-two days, Gianna sent her husband thirty-one letters, writing at least every other day. Gianna, Pierluigi, and Mariolina stayed in Magenta with Francesco and Zita while Pietro was away. Zita was a great help to Gianna, who was expecting her third child.

There are two dominant themes in these letters: the maturity of Gianna's love, and the suffering which gave new authenticity to their spousal love. Gianna and Pietro were continually discovering in one another deeper affection and devotion. This is seen not only in Gianna's letters, but also in the following letter that Pietro wrote from Germany just before his trip to the United States:

> I have always rejoiced to find in you the ideal wife of whom I had dreamed, and an incomparable mother to our children; and yet I always discover in you new virtues of sacrifice, patience, understanding, goodness, and so much loving affection. And here, far from you, your virtues are even more alive and dear to me, and I feel they are very close by *(from Stockhard, February 19, 1959).*

In addition to their forced separation, Gianna's pregnancy was a difficult one, though she tried to hide her pain from Pietro. Nevertheless, her suffering united her with her husband and with God, as she offered it to him in love.

1

Gianna worried greatly about Pietro while he traveled, especially because she was afraid of flying. She was particularly anxious when he traveled to America, since the flight was delayed and she could not receive confirmation of the flight's arrival until the morning of April 28.

Pietro wrote to Gianna immediately to send her his love and reassure her: "Thank you, my most beloved Gianna, for staying with me right up until the plane took off, in spite of your condition which calls for rest."

April 28, 1959
Tuesday, 8:30 A.M.

My dearest Pietro,

I was finally able to find out this morning that your plane reached Boston after a nine-hour delay. I had called TWA in Milan at 9:00 last night, but the latest news they had was from 3:00. You can imagine how slowly time passed while we waited. Adelaide just called to tell me your telegram from Boston had arrived. Thanks be to God! I'll wait for more detailed news; I can't write anymore now, the little ones won't leave me alone. I'll write more later when they've gone to sleep.

2 P.M.

My Pietro,

I just received your first letter that you wrote on the plane Sunday night. Thank you for your sweet words. Gigetto was pleased with his postcard and fell asleep saying, "Papa got there, Papa didn't crash." You should have heard him on Sunday when he saw the plane take off: "Ciao, Papa…Papa's in the sky…buon viaggio, Papa…Papa come back soon." Everyone around us was listening, and he explained, "Papa's up in the airplane; Papa's going far, far away…." Then, every time I called Malpensa Airport yesterday to check on your flight, he followed me, and when there was no news, he said, "Papa didn't get there," and then to console me, he said, "Mamma, Papa won't crash." What a treasure! He thought of you all day, and I had him say the "Hail Mary" and "Eternal rest…" often, his two favorite prayers that he knows by heart. Mariolina runs to the front door crying, "Papa, Papa," every time she hears the doorbell. Gigi [Gigetto], like a big man, says to her, "No, little one, Papa's far away; he'll come back tomorrow." So you can see, dearest Pietro, that you are always with us, even when there is great distance between us. The little ones keep going to the phone to call Papa…and to make them happy, I dial a number and let them talk.

Try to stay well, Pedrin *d'or*,[1] and don't wear yourself out; use some of your free time to take naps. Don't worry about me—I have plenty of help and am not at all tired.

Mr. Colombo[2] called from the Milan office today and wanted to know if he should sign your checks over to me. I told him not to, but to send me the envelope as usual. Is that okay?

Peppino Beretta's oldest daughter[3] is getting married on Saturday, May 2; the invitation came yesterday. I'm not sure what to give her. I think we gave her sister a crystal tray for her wed-

---

1. *Gianna's term of endearment for Pietro, which literally means "of gold," and may be translated as meaning "wonderful," or "as good as gold."*

2. *Mr. Colombo was La Saffa's accountant.*

3. *Giuseppe Beretta was Gianna's cousin; his daughter's name was Zita.*

ding; should I give her a set of ceramic pieces, to be different? I'll wait for your suggestions.

It's rainy and chilly here today. We turned on the heater again so the children won't be cold. They say on the radio that the bad weather is due to cold air and disturbances over the Atlantic—who knows what an awful flight you must have had! May the Lord be with you and protect you on all your other flights as well! I can only pray and give you to God's divine providence.

Ciao, my dearest husband, your little ones kiss you with all their hearts.

Affectionate big kisses from your

Gianna

Zita and Cecco greet you and remember you with all their affection.

2

April 29, 1959
Wednesday, 2 p.m.

My dearest Pietro,

I think of you as having already reached New York, though I haven't received your telegram yet. The little ones are already asleep, after hungrily eating their cereal, which was carefully prepared for them by Liberata.[1] They are a little wild today, since it's raining and they can't go outside and run around in the garden. Magenta and Ponte Nuovo are full of the measles and the chicken pox, but Pierluigi and Mariolina are still fine. Hopefully, we won't catch anything. Rita[2] has a fever, so Nando is going to San Remo again today because he's afraid it's the incubation period for the measles. I lent him your car, because his doesn't run well and his in-laws' Fiat 1400 isn't working. Mr. Crotti is driving Savina to Milan tomorrow morning at 7:00; she asked me and I didn't want to say no. She'll be back May 15. As you know, Adelaide is leaving for Lourdes tomorrow. It's too bad it's raining, because the services at Lourdes are a little sad in the rain. Mamma is fine, and she's thinking of you and sends her love.

There's nothing else new.

We are always thinking of you with great affection. Pierluigi recites a Hail Mary for his Papa every day and ends, "Papa, come back soon." Mariolina folds her little hands and blows kisses to the Blessed Mother. What treasures!

---

1. *Liberata Villa worked for the Berettas for more than fifty years.*
2. *Rita was Ferdinando and Laura Viola's third child.*

Ciao, my dearest Pietro, let me know how you're doing. Don't worry about us.

  I kiss you with all my heart, your

    Gianna

3

April 30, 1959
Thursday afternoon

My dearest Pietro,

This morning I received the letter you wrote on Monday "up in the sky," as our Gigetto says. Were you really able to sleep? I'm so glad you woke up with the sun Monday morning. You would have thought there was a tempest here, with all the rain and wind we had, so we were all very anxious until we found out from TWA that your plane had arrived safely in Boston. Gigetto is very happy because he got a letter from Papa, and he's keeping it safe in his little box along with the card from the plane.

He's as lively as ever, as is Mariolina. They couldn't sleep last night because of the storm—peals of thunder, torrents of rain, wind—it sounded like the end of the world.

They couldn't go outside today either, because of the bad weather. Patience.

I had to go to work yesterday evening and today, because I took Nando's place. He's back with Rita now, who unfortunately has the measles. She's isolated from our children, of course, and...we must hope for the best.

My Pietro, I think of you always, day and night, with so much affection, because I love you very much, you know. How nice it would be to always be together, but...let us offer everything to the Lord so that he will always help our dear and beautiful little family.

A drug salesman at the office yesterday saw the photo of our treasures and was so impressed he could not give them enough compliments, asking me what secret I had to make them grow so beautiful.

It's no secret, I told him, "God gave them to me healthy, and let's hope it stays that way," right, "paparino" of gold?

Ciao, Papa, a thousand big kisses from your Gigetto and from your beautiful little girl.[1]

Pierluigi wouldn't leave me alone; he wanted to write to his Papa.

Ciao, Pietro, take care of yourself, and don't tire yourself too much. Many greetings from Zita, Cecco, and Liberata, and most affectionate kisses from your

Gianna

---

1. This is a note from Pierluigi, who was apparently just learning to write.

❖ 4 ❖

Pietro and Gianna remained united in spirit during his long trip across the ocean. In his letter of April 27, Pietro assured Gianna of his prayers:

> Before I go to sleep I will tell Jesus, our Heavenly Mother, and our guardian angels: "Bless Gianna, and help me to always know how to make her happy. Bless the little one we are expecting with so much love and eagerness. Bless and protect Pierluigi and Mariolina, protect them from every misfortune and sickness...."

MAY 1, 1959
Friday afternoon

My dearest Pietro,

A most loving greeting today, too, even though the mail won't go out because it's May Day.

The sun has finally returned and the children are outside enjoying it, playing in the garden and running through the grass in the vineyard. I went to the office in Mesero for a little while this morning, and I took Gigetto, Mariolina, and Zita with me so that Grandma could enjoy their company for an hour or so. Flavio and Gianfranco were also there, since they're on vacation with their Grandma while Adelaide is in Lourdes.

I'm still waiting for a letter from you from New York. All I know so far is that you arrived safe and sound in Boston. We always think of you, Pedrin *d'or,* and we wish it were already the end of the month so we could go and pick you up at Malpensa. Without you, the days seem much longer and pass more slowly. But don't worry, because I'm fine. The Lord certainly hears your prayers: our treasures are in the best of health. Pierluigi went to sleep last night at 9:00 and didn't wake up until 8:30 this morning; Mariolina, on the other hand, was awake at 5:30 this morning and just had to play, no matter what.

> Dear Pedrin, a big kiss from your treasures
> and a most affectionate embrace from your
>
> *Gianna*

The following is a postscript to the letter of May 1.

May 2
Saturday

My beloved Pietro,

I received your telegram from New York this morning, thanks be to God, and thank you for sending it to me.

The children are fine. And you? Do you still have that cough? And how are your teeth? Gigi always prays that Papa's hurts will go away.

Papa, ciao, come home soon.[1]

Satisfied with his masterpiece, he's leaving me alone now. He's so mischievous, but he is in a happy mood; our little girl, on the other hand, is getting her first teeth, so she's a little cranky and doesn't sleep very much. But this disturbance will pass.

Mamma and Gina[2] had to go to Milan to pick Teresina[3] up this morning. She's been sent home because they think she might have whooping cough. The inconveniences of summer

---

1. This was written by Pierluigi.
2. Gina Gallo Garavaglia was the nurse in Gianna's practice.
3. Teresina was Pietro's niece.

camp: two contagious sicknesses in such a short time! We're staying away from Mesero—I can't tell you how hard it is to make the children understand that they can't be together!

Ciao, Papa *d'or*. A big kiss from your beautiful little treasures, and a very big one from your most affectionate

Gianna

5

MAY 4, 1959
Monday

Dearest Pietro,

I just received the letter from Boston that you wrote on the evening of the twenty-eighth. Thank you for letting me know how you are. We're all fine. The weather has calmed down and the little ones can go into the garden to enjoy the air and sun. I received the receipt for the 200 Sade shares from Bellinzaghi Bank this morning. They came with a form to send back signed, along with another form from the same bank, on which is written: Pirelli Shares & Co. Since they wanted a response by May 10, I decided to answer them myself.

I've noticed that letters take eight days to get here. I had hoped they would come more quickly than that. Patience! A whole ocean is between us! Mamma and your family are fine. Teresina is better; she doesn't have a fever. Don't get too tired, Pedrin *d'or,* and stay cheerful.

> Many big kisses from your treasures
> and a big hug from your
>
> *Gianna*

❧ 6 ❦

May 5, 1959
Tuesday

My dearest Pietro,

Pierluigi and Mariolina received your postcard of April 29 from Boston. Gigetto showed it to everyone, explaining that "up there, up there, high up in that house, Papa was sleeping." At around 5:00 this morning, he half-woke up when he heard a plane passing over, and he called to me, "Mamma, Papa's airplane is passing by"; then he went back to sleep until 8:30. Every now and then he wants his Papa, and if I tell him that Papa is far away and can't come, he answers, "He should take an airplane and come home." What ideas he has! They're both just fine: they're eating well and their color is good.

I'm anxious to hear how you are doing, if you still have that cough, and whether it is too hot over there.

There's nothing new here. Adelaide has come back [from Lourdes], but I haven't seen her yet. Mamma and Rosetta are fine too, and they say hello.

> Many big kisses from your
> treasures and from your
> *Gianna*

I just now received your long, sweet letter from Wednesday, along with the one addressed to your dear Gigetto. Thank you a million times! You can't imagine how much joy and comfort your sweet words bring me. As I have told you, your faith and piety are a great example to me—I wish I knew how to pray as you do, Pietro dear.

I urge you to stay happy, all right? Imagine that we are with you every moment of the day, and the distance will seem less to you.

> With all my love I kiss you, with your dearest little angels, your
>
> *Gianna*

Greetings from Cecco, Zita, and Savina.

7

May 6, 1959

Pietro, my darling,

I'm so happy right now because I received all the details of your trip to New York. I thank the Lord that he gave you a smooth journey. I can imagine how hard it must be to see the little polio victims. May God keep this terrible disease far from our treasures! I'm glad all your work is going well and that everyone is being so welcoming. Their kindness will make it easier to be so far from us. Is it true that everyone admires our little ones? How happy that makes me! They're so beautiful and sweet. Here in Magenta, too, people stop and look twice at them when we go out, and I do nothing but thank the Lord. I saw Adelaide this morning when I went to Ponte Nuovo to do laundry with the Bendix [washing machine]. She was all fervent and enthusiastic from her time in Lourdes; she asked me if I had gotten the tape you recorded, but I told her no. Do you think it is being held in customs?

I saw Mr. Dotto, who, as he promised, is looking after the plants and flowers in the garden. The Canossian Sisters always pray for you and they send you their greetings, so does Mother Virginia, who came to Ponte Nuovo this morning to visit the children in the nursery school.

Angela Chiolerio's father died suddenly the other night while he was writing in his study; his funeral is this afternoon. It's a relief for the family, but sorrowful because no one realized it and he died alone and without the sacraments.

Now I'm off to the office at the nursery school. I kiss you with much, much love. Take care and don't get too tired. Ten days have already gone by!

Big kisses from your little ones.

Your most affectionate
Gianna

Affectionate greetings from Cecco and Zita.

❧ 8 ❧

Gianna delighted in relating to Pietro the little everyday events of life, from her differences with Savina over disciplining and educating the children, to their outings in the country. In this letter, Gianna reminds Pietro of their first trip together to Lugano, a Swiss town about 70 kilometers from Milan. The love that was blossoming in the couple's first outing had matured and grown in their life together.

MAY 8, 1959
Friday

My dearest Pietro,

I received the long letter you sent from New York on May 4. A million thanks—even though you're tired from work and from the heat, you still manage to find time to keep me up to date every day on everything you're doing. We think about you all the time, Pedrin *d'or,* and you can imagine how happy we are reading your letters. What a hotel you're staying in! When Gigetto saw the card, he said that you are "way up high, up high, almost in the sky." I'm sorry it's so hot—it was sultry here yesterday, too. There's a breeze today though, and it feels better. Our treasures are well; they enjoy the sunshine in the vineyard almost all day long.

Angela takes really good care of them, is very attentive, and knows how to help them play. If only Savina were like that! That will take some time and patience!

I took the little ones to the cemetery in Mesero to visit their grandfather and their Aunt Teresina yesterday morning.[1] They

---

1. *Pietro's father, Luigi, died in 1956, and his sister Teresina died in 1950.*

prayed for you, with their little hands folded, that all would go well. The Lord cannot turn a deaf ear to our little angels, Pedrin *d'or.* Cecco took them to Lugano in the afternoon. So many sweet memories! I saw the long lake where you took your first picture of me at the Felix Hotel. I wish you could have been there with me again, so I could embrace you and kiss you and thank you for your great love for me and all the joys you've brought me these past three years.

The little ones had a snack and then had a great time in the park at Lugano, with the little merry-go-rounds and swings and, as always, they entertained themselves by throwing stones into the lake.

Adelaide just called to tell me the tape you recorded has arrived; they were also waiting for it in Milan.

I had to call Mr. Roveda this morning because the switch burned out on the Bendix [washing machine]. He's going to get another one when he goes to Milan. I saw the house where your offices are. It's finished, and it looks really good—it doesn't seem like the same place as before. The workers' lunchroom has been torn down. When Gigetto saw this, he said, "Mamma, Saffa fell down, you must write to Papa"—that's what he said!

Mrs. Valle wrote to ask us to let her know when we will be arriving at the "Pinto," so she can fix it up a bit before we get there. I'll send her an answer today.

Ciao darling, take care of yourself; your little ones send their most affectionate kisses.

> I embrace and kiss you with all
> my heart, your
> *Gianna*

9

May 10, 1959
Sunday, 10:00 P.M.

My dearest Pietro,

I always imagine you well and working hard, here and there. It's too bad it's so hot; here, it's gray and a little bit rainy. Father Guise is with us, enjoying our little angels for a while. He celebrated Mass at Ponte Nuovo as usual and gave a special blessing with the asperges to all his little nephews and nieces who were there. Mariolina was very good in church, but Pierluigi only stayed awake for about five minutes. After Mass, Father Guise took them to the beach we go to in Turbigo[1] while I, quite willingly, stayed home to work on the little sweater I am knitting for Alberto or Emanuela. By the way, have you thought of a name if we have a girl?

The children are asleep now. Pierluigi went to sleep at 7:00; I tried to wake him up to feed him some cereal, but he didn't want it…

Now I'm going to bed, too, since there's nothing interesting on TV—just reruns!

Ciao, darling. Big kisses from your little ones and from your most affectionate little wife.

Gianna

---

1. *Turbigo is a town on the Ticino, between Milan and Novara.*

10

May 10, 1959
Monday

My dearest Pietro,

What a wonderful day this is: I received your letter from Thursday May 7, the postcard with the cathedral like the Duomo of Milan, and Pierluigi's card with the long bridge. When he heard that you didn't have any stones to throw in the water, he took one from the garden and threw it at the postcard!

Thank you so much for letting me know how things are going. I'm sorry that you get to bed even later in order to write to me. Do you have to get up early in the morning, or can you sleep in a little bit? I'm glad your cough is gone and that your teeth are okay. Pedrin *d'or,* I wish you never had to suffer or that I could be with you when you're not feeling well. Thank you for listening to my advice not to get too tired.

The bank sent the confirmation of the acquisition of the 200 Sade shares. There's nothing else new.

I'm going to start asking you when you think you might be coming home. The mail does take three days, but it's already the eleventh.

"Papa pu [No more Papa]," says Mariolina.

"Papa will come back tomorrow," says Gigetto. In this way all of your Gigetto's other "tomorrows" will also pass until the real tomorrow comes, and we will finally be able to embrace you again.

Ciao darling, I always give your little ones big kisses from you. Take good care of yourself for me.

    A most affectionate embrace, your

      Gianna

Zita and Cecco return most cordial greetings.

❧ 11 ❧

Gianna and Pietro always expressed concern for one another's health and comfort. Gianna downplayed her sufferings, not wanting to worry her husband when he was so far away, but Pietro knew her well and read between the lines, writing to her: "And your stomach pains? Your headache? I'm sure you're not telling me about them, O my dearest wife and incomparable mother!"

May 12, 1959
Tuesday

My dearest Pietro,

I'm sending you three photos of our magnificent Mariolina, hoping they won't be too messed up by the time they reach you.

The children are fine; Gigetto plays all day long, and by 8:00 at night, he can hardly move, so he goes to sleep right away and sleeps until 8:00 in the morning. You should see what a brave little man he is when I give him a suppository or an enema for his cough. It's been a few days since he had one, so I'll give him one, but he's so good and doesn't say a word.

It's very hot here today—who knows what it must be like where you are!

I always feel the burning stomach pains, but I only have a headache every once in a while. But all this will pass and within two months we'll have our newest little one [in our arms]!

I also have a photo of your cousins here, which I'll send separately.

Take care of yourself for me, Pedrin *d'or,* and come home soon.

> Big, big kisses, lots of them, from your little ones too, your
>
> *Gianna*

12

In a conference for the young girls of Catholic Action, Gianna had written a beautiful reflection on love and marriage:

> One should not enter into marriage without knowing how to love. To love means to desire your own and your beloved's perfection, to overcome your own selfishness. Love must be total, full, complete, regulated by the law of God, and must last for all eternity in heaven.

She certainly lived out this expression of love in her marriage to Pietro, whether they were close or far away from one another.

May 13, 1959

My dearest Pietro,

The last time I heard from you was May 8—you're working as hard as ever, are tired in the evening, but you still find time to write to me. Thank you so much.

The newspaper said that two planes crashed in the United States: one New York-Atlanta flight crashed in Baltimore, the other crashed as it was coming into Kanwha (Virginia) airport, and both were Capital Airlines, four-engine planes. My Pietro, my thoughts are always with you as you travel, and I wish that the day would come quickly when you're done flying. It's a good thing Gigetto has his little triple invocation whenever he prays: "Jesus, help my Papa *have a good trip;* Papa, *come home soon;* Papa, *don't crash."* But…distance is still distance.

I was watching Father Mariano[1] on TV last night talking about true love in marriage, and he said, "true love is the love which lasts not only a day but always." He also said that spouses who have always loved each other will find out when they get to heaven that the time they have loved on earth was short, and they will rejoice to know that they have all of eternity before them to continue to love each other.

Pedrin *d'or,* you know how much I love you, how much I think of you and want to see you happy.

Come home soon, and many, many kisses from your treasures.

A most affectionate embrace from your

Gianna

---

1. *Father Mariano da Torino (1920–1972) was a Capuchin priest who was well-known for his television preaching.*

13

May 14, 1959
Thursday

My dearest Pietro,

Today I received your letters of May 10 and 11. Thank you so much. Pierluigi was all ears when I read him your letter, and when he saw that I was moved, he said, "Mamma, don't cry, Papa will come soon." And yesterday, as I was putting him to bed, he said: "My beautiful big mamma" (who taught him that, I really don't know), "I'm your big darling." What ideas he has! He's growing up so fast.

I'm sorry it's so hot there and that you have to tire yourself by traveling for hours on the train in order to make me happy. Patience, Pedrin *d'or,* but I feel better knowing you're not "in the sky." You really are a wonderful Papa. Who knows what Pierluigi will think one day when he reads your beautiful letters. Papa prays so much for his little family. Thank you for the sweet words to their mother. I will do everything I can to stay this way, as you want me to be, as you see me.

My Pietro, we're waiting anxiously to hear when you will be coming home so we can pick you up at the Malpensa Airport. And then…we'll never let you go again!

Don't worry about us, we're fine. Cecco and Zita are always eager to help and like having us here with them. They say thank you for your greetings and return heartfelt ones to you. Mamma is doing well and sends you many greetings. She goes to the cemetery to pray for you often, for her dear Pietro. Teresina is doing better: she only coughs once in awhile. Adelaide and her family are fine, too. I saw her yesterday when she gave me some chocolates and a doily from Father Felice.[1] Now I'll write to Miss Maria to thank her.

The Sisters are very happy with their piano; it's more than an octave long and it has a beautiful sound.

The new dining hall is being built very quickly. Pierluigi would stay there forever, watching the cranes moving up and down. He says that he wants to be an "engineer" just like his Papa when he grows up.

"The beautiful little one," Mariolina, is a little lady. She is never still, she laughs, she dances, makes faces, and throws a few temper tantrums.

Ciao, my beloved Pietro, take care of yourself and we hope to see you soon.

If you're tired, don't write every day.

>Many kisses from your little ones and from your most affectionate
>
>*Gianna*

---

1. *Father Felice Dominioni had been the bishop's delegate to Ponte Nuovo di Magenta until 1951.*

14

May 16, 1959
Saturday

My dearest Pietro,

I'm taking advantage of the visit of Mr. Piovesana's[1] sister-in-law from New York to send you the latest news. We are fine, the children are very lively—they're a handful, and I'm always afraid they'll hurt themselves, so I watch them constantly. The last letter I got from you was from May 11. When the mailman comes, Gigetto runs to see if "Papa writed," and he brings the letter to me all happy and satisfied, because he knows it will make me happy. And you can't imagine how happy I am to read your affectionate letters.

Now, though, I'm waiting to hear when you think you'll be coming home. It is much cooler here now, after all the storms we've been having the last few days.

"Thunder doesn't come from the wall, but from the sky," the newest statement from your little man. "I'm 'fraid," Mariolina says. What precious treasures! They're at an age when they're a lot of work, but they are wonderful with their innocent declarations.

As I write, Pierluigi is spreading out all the postcards you've sent him. "Ciao, Papa," he says while looking at the ones with airplanes, "you're already almost home." Just think of their joy when they see you again!

Come home soon, Papa, ciao.[2]

---

1. *Mr. Giuseppe Piovesana was La Saffa's general manager before Pietro.*
2. *This line was written in wobbly letters by Pierluigi.*

And your trips? You must be exhausted. Will you really fly right over the North Pole on your way back? Are you sure?

Ciao, Pedrin *d'or,* take care of yourself; we're always thinking of you.

Big kisses from your little ones, and many, many affectionate ones from

>Your
>*Gianna*

15

May 19, 1959

My dearest Pietro,

I received your letters from May 13 and 14; I hope your trip to Bridgefort went well. What skyscrapers they have in New York! It looks like a fairy kingdom with all those lights. Pierluigi is excited about his surprise. As usual, we're fine. Mariolina has been cranky the past couple of days and she doesn't want to eat, but she doesn't have a fever. Savina is back, well-rested and happy—let's hope she stays that way, because the children are calmer and happier with her this way. The weather has been nice, so they stay outside in the garden almost all day.

I'm glad to hear the factory owners you visit are so welcoming and cordial! You really deserve it, since you're always so polite and helpful to them when they come to Italy.

When I went to Ponte Nuovo this morning, I saw water dripping from the ceiling in the bathroom. The plumber said the water heater's gasket was leaking—and not only that, but the heating element was burned. He fixed everything, but I don't understand why the element burned so easily.

I saw Adelaide, and I heard your baritone voice when she played the tape on her recorder. Thank you for the greetings and the kisses.

The mayor of Milan, and most of the city council of Magenta, visited on Sunday: they toured the nursery school and visited the Sisters and the Ponte Nuovo schools. Cecco said they were very pleased, but it was a shame you weren't here to show them around.

Stay well, my Pietro, and come back soon. Wait till you see how much progress Pierluigi has made in expressing himself: he makes long, clear discourses, and repeats everything he hears with all the right words.

With all my heart I kiss and embrace you along with our treasures.

Your most affectionate
Gianna

16

May 20, 1959
Wednesday

My dearest Pietro,

Thank you, thank you, from your children too, for the wonderful surprise.

You can imagine Pierluigi's happiness at having two recordings "where Papa is talking." He wouldn't listen to anything today except your recordings. When Mariolina heard you say, "a kiss for Mariolina," she said, "Papa, Papa..."—she recognized your voice and sent you many kisses with her cute little lips. They really are a couple of treasures! And how could your good and dear little wife not be moved hearing such affectionate statements in your own voice! Thank you, Pedrin *d'or,* what a joy and comfort it is for me to know that you're thinking of me and love me so much!

Pietro wrote to Gianna:

> I served Mass at the Blessed Sacrament altar in the cathedral of New York this morning.... This evening I recited the rosary at 9:30 at the altar of the Immaculate Conception in New York.... I feel so far away from you, and my love is becoming even stronger; I feel more than ever the duty and the need to thank the good Lord morning and night.

Thursday afternoon

My dearest Pietro,

This morning I received your long letter from Saturday the sixteenth; thank God it was filled with good news. Such a wonderful and loving letter, with so many prayers for your family!

You always find time to attend Holy Mass. Unfortunately, I can never get out to it; Mariolina was awake this morning at 5:00, and I had to get up and dress her at 6:00 A.M. so she could play in the living room, otherwise, she would have awakened Pierluigi with her shrill little voice. Gigetto, on the other hand, sleeps until 8:30 A.M., since he doesn't take a nap in the afternoon anymore.

I was really hoping you would tell me that you're coming home before the end of the month…but you still don't know. Patience. Do you still have many more flights to take? Are you going to San Francisco?

Your letter from Sunday arrived, too; I enjoyed reading about the family you stayed with who admired our treasures so much.[1] I'm glad you could spend your Sunday in pleasant company.

We're all fine. Your Mamma is fine, too, and every time she sees me she asks me to say hello for her. Cecco thanks you for the stamps, and he and Zita say hello.

Dear Papa thank you for the tapes.[2]

This picture means many kisses. He wanted to write all by himself. If Gigetto is here when your letters come, I can't read them in peace, because he always wants to see them and, all seri-

---

1. *Pietro was a guest at the country home of Mr. Green, a lawyer who had business ties with La Saffa.*

2. *This was written by Pierluigi.*

ous, he reads, "Many big kisses to Gigi. Papa is still far away," etc. But now it's almost time for you to come home…don't you think?

Ciao Pedrin *d'or,* take care of yourself; I kiss you with all my affection.

Thank you for everything, your
Gianna

❖ 17 ❖

Pietro wrote in his letter of Saturday, May 16: "I hope to be able to tell you within the coming week the exact week of my return, if not the exact day. I'm trying to hurry, but the five-day work week and the long trips from one city to another make the weeks slip by too quickly."

May 22, 1959
Friday

My dearest Pietro,

I have here your little note from Monday the eighteenth at 11:30 P.M.—you must be so tired, and you had to leave right away again on Tuesday morning! I still haven't gotten a letter from you saying, "I've finished my work…I'll meet you on such and such a day, at such and such time." Sadly, you still don't know. It's been twenty-six days since you left, and it seems like you've been so far away for months and months. Gigetto always says, "Papa isn't coming back, he's far, far away," and you still have to take such long flights.

We're still staying with Zita, though tomorrow I'll have to spend the night at Ponte Nuovo because I'm having the mattresses redone on all the beds.

Two Englishmen conducted a detailed inspection at the plastic laminates plant—rumors were flying. Zita said that the only news so far is that the lawyer Zaninoni no longer introduces himself as a lawyer, but as "Mr. Zaninoni." Mr. Notari, the engineer, asked when you would be coming back—I don't know why.[1]

---

1. *Zaninoni was the general manager of the laminated plastics branch of La Saffa, and Notari was La Saffa's manager.*

Cecco said that Mr. Denotti, the engineer, provided some panels for the school's open house; he must have asked the higher-ups about it before Cecco wrote you. Everyone is busy preparing for Magenta's June festival.[2] Almost all of the houses are being painted…you wouldn't believe the colors—the most common is yellow, in a variety of shades.

The front of the church is finished, and the scaffolding is down; it's very beautiful and imposing. Monsignor [Luigi Crespi] is very satisfied with the result, and is often seen contemplating it.

Bellinzaghi Bank sent us some letters about the Pirelli shares; there's no reply deadline, so I thought you might be back in time to answer them, because I honestly don't understand very much about it.

Gigetto is very happy today because his new record, "All the Mothers," has finally arrived. He loves his music passionately—watch out if he can't play his records for some reason! He knows your tape messages by heart and repeats them even before you speak. Both of them are doing very well: no sign of the measles, thank God.

Teresina has recovered completely, but now Luigino is sick with whooping cough.

Mamma is fine; she always asks me for news about you.

In the hope of seeing you soon, with all my love I kiss and embrace you, with our treasures.

Your most affectionate
Gianna

---

2. *The June festival was in remembrance of the Battle of Magenta (June 1859).*

❧ 18 ❧

Gianna's letters were filled with her daily life and cares: she moves quickly from anxiety over the upcoming birth, sadness at Pietro's absence, expressions of love, and her consistent faith and trust in God, to delight in telling her husband about their children and the joy in their lives.

MAY 24, 1959
Sunday

My beloved Pietro,

It's 3:00 P.M., and our little angels have gone to Legnano[1] with their aunts, Angela, and Savina; Mr. and Mrs. Viola invited them there to see the floats at the festival. I preferred to stay at home where it's quiet, since the ninth month starts today and I get tired easily. All alone and with much emotion, I read and re-read the sweet letters you've sent me so faithfully every day from America. I am in your dear company, feeling better today... but yesterday, I will admit, I was a bit down. I wanted you here with me, and I missed you so much that I decided to write and tell you to come home right away. But the feeling passed.... Today I say, "Come home as soon as possible, Pedrin *d'or,* as soon as you can."

Last night, before going to sleep, Gigetto said to me, "Mamma, I want to see my Papa. He's still so far away, he's never coming back!" What a darling, he loves you so much and misses

---

[1]. *Legnano is a town near Milan, about 16 km north of Magenta. Each year, on May 29, there is a parade to celebrate the town's victory in a battle against Emperor Frederick Barbarossa in 1176.*

you… "Papa has to fix my little red car…my tricycle…etc. I'm going up in the sky so I can see my Papa!" and so on; it's one statement after another, as if he were already grown up. Mariolina is as wild as ever, and she does everything that Gigetto does, so they often end up quarreling. They are doing very well and, thanks to your prayers, there have been no "misfortunes."

My cousin Piera had her baby and they named her Simonetta. Piera is still in the hospital, though, because they had to do a C-section, I'm not sure why. But she's all right and hopes to go home within the week. What a thought, though…I trust in Our Lady, and I'm sure that she will help me this time, just as she did before. The prayers of my dearest and most loving Pietro are too many for her not to. Thank you for everything, Pedrin *d'or,* for your great love for me and for our treasures, for your fatigue and all your hard work, and for all your sacrifices.

I hope it's not too hot where you are. It's been rainy and chilly here for the past few days, with a little bit of clearing in between. I'm glad it's been cool, because the heat would be too much for me.

Archbishop Montini[2] will be here on June 2 for the opening of the front of the Basilica; the schools will be closed and the preparations for the ceremony are underway.

I hope I'll receive word of the day of your return tomorrow.

I kiss you again and again with all my heart, and our dear treasures kiss you with me.

Ciao, my Pietro, come back soon,

your
Gianna

---

2. *Archbishop Giovanni Battista Montini, the future Pope Paul VI, was archbishop of Milan until after Gianna's death.*

19

MAY 25, 1959
Monday evening

My dearest Pietro,

Our dear little ones have been asleep for three hours already, like two little angels, tired out after running and playing in the vineyard. If you could only see Pierluigi's energetic somersaults! He's better at it than his cousins, and Mariolina follows him around and tries to do everything he does. So when nighttime comes, they're tired and fall asleep in two minutes.

I got your letter of Thursday the twenty-first this afternoon. I can't deny, Pedrin *d'or,* that when I read you wouldn't be back until June 10, I got very depressed. I had a good cry…then I offered this sacrifice to the Lord for you so that he might protect you during all your trips, and for the baby we are expecting, so it will be born beautiful and healthy. And so, I resigned myself. I gave Gigetto and Mariolina many kisses, pressed them to my heart, and with them, I felt you very close to me, as if you were already here with us.

Try not to get too tired, my Pietro; if all your days are as busy as Wednesday was, I can imagine how exhausted you must be every night. Yet, you still manage to send me your loving words. I will always be grateful to you, my husband and Papa *d'or!*

Pierluigi came into our room in Ponte Nuovo this morning and, seeing our engagement photo, said, "…Papa, Papa, he's back, look, I saw Papa…." He didn't know how to show his joy at seeing you—he pressed the picture to his heart…what a beautiful child! One cannot help but to be touched by his displays of affection!

Going back to your flights, are the two-engine planes safe? Excuse my ignorance, but it seems to me a four-engine plane could better handle the air pockets, etc. I was happy to hear that you had an enchanting trip, though, sitting close to the pilot, and close to heaven! And since we are always close to you, it's almost as if we are also enjoying the beautiful things you tell us about.

I don't think Foster Dulles' death will prevent you from working, but I hope the factories don't close, otherwise June 10…might turn into June 20![1]

Ciao, my Pietro, don't worry about us, we're fine.

> Big, big kisses, and many of them from your treasures and from your most affectionate
>
> *Gianna*

---

1. John Foster Dulles (1888–1959) was President Eisenhower's Secretary of State.

20

May 26, 1959
Tuesday

Dearest Pietro,

A loving little greeting today, too, from your wife and from your little ones, who, thanks be to God, are fine even though everywhere in Ponte Nuovo there are cases of measles, and whooping cough and scarlet fever in Magenta. I only take the children out in the car, and after all, they do like playing in the garden and in the vineyard just as much as going out. Zita and Cecco want us to stay here, rather than going back to Ponte Nuovo, because they say the children are already used to it here and it would be a shame to take them away. My Pietro, I hope June 10 comes quickly—very quickly! My longing to see and embrace you again is too much! Don't forget—June 14 is the feast of Ponte Nuovo and Bishop Pignedoli[1] will be visiting and administering Confirmation and Communion. You'll be here, right?

Mamma is fine, and so are your sisters and their families. Ciao, beautiful Pedrin, take care and don't get too tired.

> Big kisses from your little angels and a most affectionate embrace from your
>
> *Gianna*

---

1. Bishop Sergio Pignedoli was the auxiliary bishop of Milan at the time.

❦ 21 ❧

Pietro often had trouble with his teeth, and had to go to an American dentist to have a tooth pulled. Gianna was somewhat shocked at his having to go to an American, especially since Pietro recounted his visit with a comical twist in order to downplay the drama.

On May 27, Pietro had to leave on a 15-day trip to Cincinnati, Chicago, and California, which prevented him from receiving Gianna's letters regularly.

MAY 27, 1959
Wednesday

My dearest Pietro,

I was so sorry to hear about your toothache; you did the right thing by having it pulled. I can't believe you had to have it done in America! If I even had to go to the dentist in Mesero—you can imagine. Let's hope you won't have any more trouble with it.

When Pierluigi heard you had to have a tooth pulled, he immediately told everyone—his uncle, his aunt—"Poor Papa, he had a tooth pulled, he had to have a shot and they put a bandage around his head!" He just finished pretending to be Modugno,[1] with his arms opened wide, moving his legs just like Modugno does. He had another revelation last night: "Mamma, when I'm big, I'll go to school with Iucci and Toia; then when I come home, I'll say, 'Ciao, Mariolina, I'm back!'" He is already so big, very mischievous and always on the move. Mariolina

---

1. *Domenico Modugno was a popular singer in Italy at the time; one of his most famous songs was "Volare."*

watches the other kids riding their bikes and tries as hard as she can to follow them on her tricycle—and she's only a year and a half old!

I'm sorry that you won't be able to hear from us for two weeks because of your traveling away from New York, but these wanderings of yours will end, and you won't have to go away on other trips again, as you told me the evening of the concert, right? I put my foot down…no, just kidding, not I, but the third baby.

My Pietro, I can imagine how much you want to come back to us, but patience! The Lord asks us for this sacrifice. He is so good to us! We're all doing well, and the children become more beautiful every day.

The historical display[2] will be opened by the authorities in Milan tomorrow. The panels you ordered with the history of Milan are at the plastics plant, but no one knows where to put them—not even Mr. De Noti.

Ciao, Pedrin *d'or,* take good care of yourself; your little ones send you many kisses with their little lips and their little hands.

An affectionate embrace from your wife who always thinks of you and who loves you very, very much. Hope to see you soon,

your
Gianna

Zita, Cecco, Liberata, Angela, and Savina return heartfelt greetings to you.

---

2. The historical display was in commemoration of the 100th anniversary of the Battle of Magenta, when the Franco-Sardinian troops commanded by Napoleon defeated the Austrians. This was a significant step toward the unification of Italy.

22

May 29, 1959
Friday

My dearest Pietro,

The last letter I got from you was from May 24; I was hoping to receive something today, but I think the mail takes longer to get here since you're traveling. I trust in the Lord, however, and think of you as tired, but in good health, without toothaches or headaches. We are just fine here.

I took the children to see the procession for the feast of Corpus Christi yesterday: banners, little girls dressed in white—it was a real treat for them. The historical display at the Giacobbe House was also opened yesterday, and the ceremony was broadcasted on TV in the evening; 200 important people from Milan were there. Cecco said both the ceremony and the display came off very well, very interesting—partly due to you, Pedrin *d'or*.[1]

In twelve days, we'll all be together again. You can imagine how I'm counting the days and the hours, along with Gigetto, who keeps asking me, "When is Papa coming home?" You've never been gone this long before.

Tomorrow afternoon, Mr. Crotti will take Zita, Gigetto, and I to Milan to buy a few little things for the children; Piera will be expecting us a 4:30 p.m. at Aunt Virginia's house for Simonetta's baptism.

---

1. Pietro had come up with the idea of the panels and had brought the idea to fruition.

Piera is fine now, but she suffered a lot; she says she's forgotten all that, though, because Simonetta is such a wonderful baby. The Lord consoles mothers quickly, doesn't he? Mamma, Zita, and Cecco send you their affectionate greetings, and they think of you often.

Ciao, dear husband, how much I want you!

I kiss you with your treasures, and I embrace you affectionately,

your
Gianna

23

May 31, 1959
Sunday

My dearest Pietro,

Thank you for your greetings in your own voice. I went to your office yesterday with Mariolina and Gigetto to listen to your tape. It's too bad the machine makes your voice sound more baritone, so the children weren't really sure it was you. They loved how you made the tape with words and music, though; they'll understand even more when they're older. I also received your letter from Monday the twenty-fifth, the night before you left New York; it's a good thing these are the last ten days and that…they, too, will pass.

We're waiting to hear when we should come pick you up at Malpensa. Each evening, before he goes to sleep, Pierluigi sends you a kiss with his little hand and says, "Baby Jesus, take this kiss to my Papa." I bought him his first little suit jacket in Milan yesterday—you should see what a big boy he is! (He wears the size of a four-year-old.) Now, when he gets himself dressed, he looks at himself in the mirror and comments, "How nice, I look nice." I tell you! This morning, he just had to go to Mass, no matter what: "I'm big now. I'll be good." After Mass, we all went with Zita to visit Aunt Ginia. She's a little tired, but her spirits are good. She's waiting for Father Alberto, so she can ask his advice. His companions are already arriving, but he is only flying as far as Portugal, so that he can visit Fatima and Lourdes before returning in August. That's what one of the Franciscan brothers on Monfort Street told Father Giuse. I sent a letter to Grajau, and now I'm waiting for an answer.

Another notice from Bellinzaghi Bank arrived for the Edison shares. I have to respond by June 8. Every nine of the old shares yielded one of 2,000 lire. I will answer yes. What do you think? It's always better to buy them; the old shares are 288, so the new ones would be thirty-two.

Ginia, Nando, and Aunt Piera thank you for the greetings you sent them, they return them sincerely and they all hope everything is going well for you.

Beautiful Pedrin, don't worry about us, because we're fine. Have a good trip and don't get too tired—if you don't manage to do everything, don't worry, because you have already done so much that your bosses can't help but be pleased.

The Englishmen are still visiting the laminates plant: Dr. Bottoni showed two of them around the other day, and the lawyer was with Conte Gerli yesterday. The rumor is that the Englishmen want to do business with La Saffa and they want you as director.

Ciao my Pietro, I kiss you with all my heart and I embrace you with all my love, together with your treasures,

your
Gianna

❧ 24 ❧

JUNE 1, 1959
Monday

My dearest Pietro,

I just received your cards from last week and the letter about formica that you wrote on the plane. You really are more in heaven than on earth when you travel! And how much distance you cover in just a few hours! We think of you constantly and accompany you with our prayers, hoping this really will be our last week away from each other. I'm glad everyone is welcoming you so courteously. Zita says nobody knows what's going on at the laminates plant.

Two invitations came for you: one for tomorrow's inauguration of the basilica, the other for Thursday, June 4. I passed both of them on to La Saffa; Mr. Tarsi will probably go.

Thanks to you, the historical display is extremely popular, for its content as well as its elegance. There are always crowds of people going to see it.

We're all fine here. I always have the burning stomach pains, but at least I have some suffering to offer the Lord for you, dear Pietro, so you come back safe and sound—and soon. Our marvelous little "devils" play in the garden all day long. They're eating well and sleeping. They send their hellos and kisses to any airplane that passes overhead.

Ciao, my Pietro, thank you for always giving me news of where you are and what you are doing; I anxiously and joyfully await your letters.

Big, big kisses, your
Gianna

25

June 2, 1959
Tuesday

My dearest Pietro,

It's 9:00 P.M.; our treasures have already been asleep for half an hour. They went to bed because they just couldn't keep their eyes open. They're so active, and it's a good thing they have guardian angels—what one doesn't do the other dreams up. Let's hope that they'll calm down a little as they get older.

There was a big celebration to welcome Archbishop Montini today. I didn't go, but Zita said there were a lot of people. Even now, I can hear people passing by on their way to the church, because there's a solemn procession with the urn of sacred Chrism, something that hasn't happened in a long time.

Tomorrow morning at 8:00, Mr. Crotti is going to take Mamma and Teresina to Monza to pick up Sister Luigia [Pietro's sister] and take her to the station. As usual, she came to bring back some children and pick up others. She told me on the phone that she's doing all right, though she's a little tired.

And you? Who knows where you might be right now.

I'm waiting for a postcard from San Francisco, the last, long leg of your trip.

Everyone here is asking when you'll be back.

Ten more days, my Pedrin, and then…enough of your being away! You'll be all ours.

Big kisses from your treasures; take care, don't get too tired.

A big hug from your most affectionate

Gianna

26

June 3, 1959
Wednesday

My dearest husband Pietro,

I just received your postcards and letters from Chicago—how can I thank you for not letting a day go by without sending me word? The children are pleased with their cards, and are very happy because Papa is coming home soon. I'm glad to hear that you'll begin your return trip on Tuesday, or at least start moving back in our direction.

Thanks be to God! May the Lord accompany you, as usual, in your travels.

We're all fine. After we do some housecleaning, we'll return to "home base" next week, to wait for the return of our dearest and most beloved Papa.

It's not too hot right now, and we hope you're not suffering too much from the heat.

I'm glad you're well, with no toothaches, and that your stomach isn't giving you problems.

Many greetings from Cecco and Zita.

>Big, big kisses from your treasures and from your most affectionate
>
>*Gianna*

27

June 4, 1959
Thursday

Dearest Pietro,

I received your telegram from San Francisco this week: you're still having a good trip, thanks be to God! I just can't stand it anymore—I can't wait for you to come home; only when you're here with us will I be happy and…calm. I'm glad you got our letters in San Francisco.

Dr. Portel's[1] sister called to give me news of you and convey your greetings. I can imagine how hot it must be in California. It's been hot here, too, for the last couple of days: it was 80 degrees here today! The children are sweating and drinking a lot, but they're fine.

They enjoyed seeing the parade this morning, with all the bands and banners, etc. Now they're sleeping like two little angels.

Mamma was able to spend some time with Sister Luigia yesterday; she's doing really well and thanks you from Sister Rosina for calling her brother. I think when Sister Luigia read Sister Rosina the letter in which you told her that you spoke with him, Sister Rosina fainted with emotion and joy.

It's 11:00 P.M. now, and I can hear loud bangs from the sports field—it's the fireworks. I wanted to bring the children to see them, but it's very late for them. I don't think they've heard it yet.

Which route are you taking home? Are you stopping in Paris, too? My dearest Pietro, I can imagine how much you miss

---

1. Dr. Portel Armando was a doctor in Magenta.

us and how anxious you are to come home. Can't you skip any stops?

I have to go to the children—they're waking up, frightened and calling to me.

There, now they're asleep again; the fireworks are over.

On his flight to Los Angeles on May 31, Pietro wrote:

> Jesus, who created me and who sustains me with unlimited graces and blessings…you, who have given me the immense gift of a wife of gold like that of the most marvelous dawn, which one can only rightly admire from above, and two treasures as splendid as the heavens in all their glory, which can only be embraced on high…you who, in a short time, will repeat your divine gift with another treasure, hear my prayer. Bless Gianna and our treasures! Change into grace the anxiety and fear of my being so far away and of flying so often.

In this same letter, he described the wonder of flying over the Rocky Mountains and the Grand Canyon. Gianna responded to his letter with equal emotion…

Friday

I received your postcards and the magnificent prayer you wrote on the flight to Los Angeles. I love hearing about the wonders of nature; your descriptions remind me of those films we saw together at the Manzonis', remember?

We remember you in our prayers and always think of you.

Ponte Nuovo is still full of the measles, so I'm waiting till next week to bring the children home. Your treasures kiss you with love.

Gigi is impatient—he wants to go mail the letter to his Papa. It's his "job": when he escorts Zita to the plant at 1:30 P.M., he goes to the post office with Cecco to drop the letter off.

Many greetings from Mamma, Zita, and Cecco.

Big, big kisses, your
Gianna

You really are the dearest and most affectionate husband, a saintly Papa, not of gold, but of diamond, the biggest and most precious one there is on earth! Ciao, darling, we'll see each other soon.

28

June 6, 1959
Saturday

My dearest Pietro,

You can't imagine how we're counting the days till you come home. I imagine you're already on your trip back to New York before you return to Italy.

"Papa is coming back soon," Gigi tells everyone, and he can't wait till we can go to pick you up at Malpensa. He wakes up every morning and asks, "Mamma, is Papa coming today?" Mariolina waves to you with her little hand when airplanes go by.

It's still pretty hot here; how is it there? I think we'll have to send [the children] to Courmayeur before the end of the month.

Mrs. Valle still hasn't answered the letter I wrote her a month ago, but that's how she does things.

We're all fine, and so is your family. Mamma was pleased to hear that you visited her relatives [in Lincoln, Nebraska].

Ciao, Pedrin *d'or,* take care of yourself and we'll hopefully see you soon; big kisses from your little ones and from your most affectionate

Gianna

29

June 7, 1959
Sunday

My dearest Pietro,

It's 4:00 P.M. and while our treasures are out playing in the garden, I can't deny that I'm feeling a little sad as I think about last Sunday at 4:00 P.M.[1] Pietro, we're so far apart, and it takes so long for the mail to get here! Then I start thinking that my letters won't reach you at all, or if you do get them, the news will already be old. My thoughts are always with you, especially when you're flying; things are always happening, and we read about air disasters almost every day. I won't say anything more; I'm praying and trusting in the Lord.

Zita and I brought the children to see Mother Virginia in Milan this week; she was able to visit with us for a couple of hours. The children put on quite a show: playing, dancing, singing. Rita seems to be over the measles, and Nando thinks it must be an allergic kind, but we are still keeping the children separated, just in case.

Pierluigi loves talking about his Papa—today, he helped me clean the living room, since "his Papa" is supposed to arrive. Every time he hears a plane, he looks up at the sky and says to you, "Ciao, Papa, come home soon," and Mariolina also waves her little hand, saying, "Papa, Papa!" Gigi wants the kisses his Papa sends him from far away in the evening: one on the forehead, one on the cheeks, and one on the lips; what an angel!

---

1. Gianna had not been well the previous Sunday.

Beautiful Pedrin, now here are many, many kisses from your Gianna who loves you very much, who thinks of you and wants you to always be happy.

With all my love, I embrace you,

Gianna

❖ 30 ❖

From California, Pietro wrote: "I felt myself very close to all of you in the quiet church with the same crucified Jesus, the same Immaculate Mother, the same St. Joseph, and the same St. Francis of Assisi as our churches have."

JUNE 8, 1959
Monday

My dearest Pietro,

I'm hoping that by the time this letter reaches New York, you will already be on your way home. Gigetto is here and he won't let me write in peace: "I want to write, too," he keeps saying. He had a high fever and sour breath on Saturday, but it passed quickly and by Sunday he was as lively and mischievous as ever. Because of the heat, they've been drinking a lot, and come to think of it, I think it was too much water that made him sick. He's waiting for his Papa, and he wants a big iron wagon, a little tricycle, and a big car like [his cousin] Alberto for his name day.[1] What big dreams he has!

Yesterday was the soldiers' holiday in Magenta, so they marched in formation down the street, with much fanfare. You can picture the children at the window, enjoying the spectacle; then, at 5:00 P.M., the *Giro d'Italia* [Italian Bikers' Tour] passed by and the street was filled with bicycles, motorcycles, cars. A helicopter even landed near our vineyard. Gigetto thought it was your plane: "Papa's come, here in our garden."

---

1. Pierluigi's name day was the feast of St. Aloysius, on June 21.

Dearest Pietro, I don't know how to thank you for the wonderful and affectionate letters that you send me every day, telling of your love for me and your dearest treasures, words that mirror your good, sweet soul, your big heart, your faith, your spirit of prayer.

Thank you, thank you with all my heart for everything. Waiting to embrace you, I kiss you with much, much love,

your

Gianna

Ciao, Papa, Gigi and Mariolina are waiting for you and kiss you very hard![2]

---

2. *Written by Pierluigi.*

❧ 31 ❧

June 9, 1959
Tuesday

My dearest Pietro,

I had been hoping to receive the telegram saying, "I will arrive Thursday the eleventh," but instead, you won't be coming until Tuesday. Always *fiat!* Your Mamma told me yesterday that I shouldn't let you go, that I should forbid it. "That's a lot of hot air," I told her. "It's part of his job." But I said to myself, "Enough Saffa, leave him alone for a while—he's already done enough!" And then today I received your letter of June 4, in which you tell me you won't be home till the fourteenth.

Poor Pedrin, I'm sorry about the heat and temperature changes; they certainly can't be good for you.

Flavio was waiting [to be confirmed] because he wanted you to be his sponsor. I'm thinking of giving him a watch as a gift—I'll go to see Mr. Pozzi.

We're all fine. Gigetto is all better after Saturday's indisposition. He's very thirsty all the time, but it's very hot (as high as 86 degrees sometimes); it feels like the sultry days of July.

I'm enclosing a newspaper clip about the laminates plant from today's *Corriere della Sera*.

Bishop Pignedoli will arrive Sunday morning at 7:45 for the First Communion Mass at 8:00. At the end of Mass the sponsors for Confirmation will come forward. There will be a procession at 4:00, just like every year.

My Pietro, do you remember the feast of Ponte Nuovo in 1955? It was the first time I went to your house—how much we already loved each other! It's because our love is so great that this separation is such a great sacrifice.

May the Lord accompany you on the flights you still have to take.

Not a day passes when your treasures don't ask about you. Mamma says hello as usual and sends you very affectionate greetings; she is very well and is no longer tired.

I kiss you with much, much love until I can embrace you again and press you to my heart.

Your most affectionate
Gianna

Pietro returned to his family on Wednesday, June 17, 1959. On June 15, Gianna was taken to the hospital in a great deal of pain, as she described in a letter to her friend Mariuccia:

> A month ago, I had to be rushed to the hospital because of toxemia. I had terrible pains, continuous contractions, fever, and vomiting. I ran the risk of losing the baby. Thoroughly frightened, I obeyed Nando and let myself be brought to [the hospital at] Monza. It was midnight, and an obstetrician I know well was waiting for me. With oxygen, sedatives, and hypodermics, the crisis passed. Two days later, I was able to go to Malpensa Airport to meet Pietro who, unaware of what had happened, was returning from the United States.

On July 15, less than a month after Pietro's return, Laura was born into the Molla family.

❖ PART IV ❖

The Last Letters

JUNE 1960–FEBRUARY 1961

After his trip to the United States in 1959, Pietro spent less time away from his family. Gianna even traveled with him on two of his business trips. Thus, these last letters are fairly brief, filled with everyday concerns, such as grocery lists and instructions on the care of the children, as well as Gianna's expressions of undiminished love and tenderness for her husband and children.

❧ 1 ❧

Once again, the Mollas spent the summer in Courmayeur, though this time they rented a villa from the Coltellis in Verrand, instead of their usual vacation house owned by Mrs. Valle.

June 27, 1960
Monday evening

My dearest Pietro,

We've arrived and are all settled into our "cute" little house, as Mariolina called it. The weather is beautiful, so the children stay outside in the meadow all day long.

Lauretta is already doing better: she has some color and is eating well. She didn't take a nap again today, so she was in bed this evening by 8:00; she's sharing a room with Mariolina, who is very happy to have her little sister for company. Gigetto, on the other hand, only just went to bed, and so everything is quiet. Dear Pietro, how beautiful it is to be able to stay with them day and night, to watch and enjoy them all of the time. I can imagine how disappointed you must be when you come home in the evening and they're already in bed. It doesn't seem real to them to have their Mamma all to themselves all of the time. Gigetto—maybe because he's going to preschool—does nothing but call to me, and he would like nothing better than to have me all to himself.

They're really three treasures; it's too bad my fourth treasure, my beloved and affectionate Pietro, is missing. I think of you all the time, and I'm close to you in my heart, with my prayers. Don't get too tired, do you understand? Go to bed early—I go to bed by 10:00, if not earlier. Last night we were all asleep by 9:30.

Thank you for your phone calls; Pierluigi insists on staying up until you call, because, he says, "I must talk to my Papa."

Here is a list for you when you come: apples, oranges, bananas, 2 kg of meat (the kind I usually get in Mesero), a pillow for Gigetto, because the ones here are too high for him, old records in the red bag for Mariolina—33 rpm records, your overcoat, a feather pillow for you, and a high chair.

It might be good if you could drive the Fiat 600, if it's there, and come with Mr. Crotti in two cars, so that I can keep one here to take the children out.

That's all for now. Don't worry about us because we're doing fine. Gianfranco is looking out for Gigetto like a guardian angel. Hello to Mamma, Adelaide, and everyone from all of us. A big hug and a big kiss for you from your treasures and from your most affectionate

Gianna

2

July 4, 1960
Monday evening

My dearest Pietro,

Our treasures are asleep, peaceful and happy—happy because of the magnificent little house their Papa found for their vacation. Pierluigi and Mariolina are two "big kids," sleeping by themselves. When they wake up in the morning, they talk and tell each other stories, happy in their little beds with the blue bedspreads. Pierluigi keeps his little glow-in-the-dark statue of Our Lady of Lourdes on his night table, and woe to his sisters if they dare to touch it! They play in the garden all day, sometimes with little stones, sometimes with their Legos; later in the day, I take them to Verrand, with Savina, up where it's safe. Laura and the children arrived today; Pierluigi, Mariolina, and Lauretta enthusiastically showed them every corner of the house, inside and out. You should have seen them, the little treasures; it's so true that beautiful sunshine and a happy atmosphere makes even the children more serene; they enjoy it so much. It's all because of you, Papa, your treasures and I thank you over and over again.

I think of you every moment, in your travels and your work, and I am very close to you with all my affection and love.

We'll be waiting for you on Saturday—come early in the evening, not late.

Big kisses from your dearest little ones and many, many affectionate ones from your

Gianna

❧ 3 ❧

Pietro had to make a short business trip to Stockhard, Germany, while Gianna stayed in the mountains with the children. Shortly after Pietro's return to his family, Gianna would have to return to Magenta for a time for her medical practice, while Pietro stayed with the children.

JULY 6, 1960
Wednesday evening

My dearest Pietro,

I'm glad your trip went well, and it was good to hear from you, but you seemed very tired. You really need a few weeks of complete relaxation. How can you go on like this?

It's so beautiful to spend the entire day with our treasures. They are calmer these days, but I have to watch them and keep them from quarreling.

We walked down to Pré-Saint-Didier to get the [gas] coupons,[1] but the Coltellis had not notified the office, so we couldn't get any. I called Mrs. Coltelli and she assured me that her husband would take care of it when he goes to town tomorrow. If you pass by Pré-Saint-Didier on Saturday and feel like stopping, you can pick them up yourself.

You should see how Lauretta is walking without any help at all. Today, I bought all three of them a pair of tennis shoes because they needed them.

Today was a beautiful day, and there is a serene, star-filled sky this evening.

---

1. In order to promote tourism, the government provided coupons for gasoline.

Here is a list of what we need:

1. an iron, the light one we always use;
2. the orange juicer;
3. the big oval skillet (shallow) for steaks—the stainless steel one;
4. salad servers;
5. ask Adelaide for a skein of white yarn to finish the baby's sweater;
6. a kitchen calendar (to keep track of how much milk we buy every day);
7. 3 kg. oranges, 3 kg. apples, 1 kg. bananas from the fruit vendor in Boffalora.[2]

Please put everything in a suitcase, since I'll need one for going home.

Ciao Pedrin, I'm sorry if the list is a little long; I hope it doesn't take up too much of your time.

We'll be waiting for you—you can imagine how excitedly.

Greetings to Mamma, Adelaide, and the nephews.

A big kiss from your little ones who are sound asleep; thank you for your ever-affectionate greetings from Stockhard.

A big hug from your
Gianna

---

2. *Boffalora Ticino was just a few kilometers from Ponte Nuovo.*

4

The date of this letter is uncertain, though it was most likely written on either July 7 or 8, before Pietro returned from Germany.

JULY 1960

My dearest Pietro,

Thank you for your loving greetings. I return them with all my heart, along with many kisses from your little ones. When Lauretta wakes up in the morning, she calls, "Papa, Papa!" What a treasure! The poor thing still has a little bit of a cough. Last night, Gigetto sounded like he was starting to get whooping cough, and today he coughed twice more. Patience, let's hope medicine and fresh mountain air will help avoid a really bad case.

The weather is terrible today—it's cold and cloudy, but we can still go higher in the mountains, since we have the car.

We'll be waiting for you excitedly on Saturday afternoon; come as early as you can.

I'll need some wine and the two salamis that are still there, and oranges and apples; I'll buy the meat. Nothing else at the moment.

Thank you for the two wonderful photos: imagine how nice they would be if they were in color! The money you sent is more than enough.

Ciao, Pedrin *d'or,* take care of yourself, don't work too hard, and we'll see you Saturday. Big kisses from all of us and hello to Mamma.

Your most affectionate
Gianna

5

Gianna wrote this letter from Magenta, where she was working in her medical practice.

July 12, 1960
Tuesday

Dearest Pietro,

I'm sending you some suppositories for Gigetto. Give him one in the morning when he wakes up and one in the evening before he goes to bed. When he takes a nap at 2:00 P.M., give him a Guajakirsch suppository.

I went to the nursery school this morning to tell the Sisters that I'm getting vaccinations for all the children; unfortunately, many children have the same type of cough that Gigetto has. It's a good thing our children are already in the mountains, since they can get better more quickly there. I'm fine; after sleeping for ten hours last night, my headache is gone. I'm here, but my thoughts are always with you, my dearest treasures.

Hopefully, I'll arrive late on Saturday with Zita; her new boss, an engineer from the Alcha Company (I think that's spelled right), is arriving Saturday, perhaps with a new manager for the firm, but nothing is certain yet.

I'm sending you an express delivery that arrived this morning; I'll bring a registered letter that came from Bellinzaghi Bank when I come.

Kiss the children for me and let me know how they are; hello to everyone and a big hug for you,

your
Gianna

For the aerosol bottle, buy an injectable bottle of strepto-chemicitine; dilute it with the little vial that's attached to the bottle, plus a vial from the red box that is on the buffet, and give it to him twice a day; if there's any liquid left in the aerosol bottle, change it and rinse it with water before using it again.

Thank you, Pietro; I don't want him to get whooping cough. Kisses to everyone, especially Lauretta on Friday morning [for her birthday]. Don't let the cousins come over; have a party at home with cake and candles. I embrace you and we'll see you Saturday.

6

Gianna wrote this postcard to Pietro for the children.

February 14, 1961

To the engineer Dr. Pietro Molla
Saffa, Ponte Nuovo, Magenta
(Milan)

Dearest Papa,

Thank you for your card, your thoughts, and all your loving words. We are sorry you're not here with us to enjoy the warm sun and beautiful snow in Courmayeur! We are having so much fun. Thank you, Papa, for having brought us up here! Many kisses from all of us, Mamma too, and we'll see you Saturday.

Your three treasures

7

From Courmayeur
FEBRUARY 4, 1961
Tuesday evening

My dearest Pietro,

Our three dearest treasures are asleep, after having walked, played, and skied all day—they were tired tonight. Afterward, Pierluigi didn't want to eat and just drank a little tea.

Tomorrow, I'll keep them in the yard so they won't get so tired.

I hope the weather stays as nice as it has been: it's calm and the sun is warmer than in July, and the mountains look bright and clean, even more beautiful than in the summer.

All the women are sunbathing at Checrouit, while the children fly down the hills on their skis and sleds like perpetual motion machines.

Lauretta wouldn't leave me again today; she's still getting used to the new surroundings.... Mariolina, on the other hand, gracefully plows through the snow in her boots.

As I told you on the phone, Pierluigi is having a ball with his sled and isn't a bit afraid of going down the hill by himself; he trudges back up, pulling his sled, and after about an hour of doing this, he sits down and says, "I've played a lot today."

Too bad it's [the sledding hill] twenty minutes away; it would be so much easier if it were right outside the house.

My Pietro, how often I think of you and how I wish you were here with us! Thank you for everything, Pedrin *d'or:* for your great love, your care, for all your goodness. Your treasures kiss you with all their love, and so does your most affectionate
Gianna

❧ CONCLUSION ❧

"God is love: whoever remains in love dwells in God and God dwells in him" (1 Jn 4:16). For the Christian, God's very nature is love: the incandescent fire that gives joy and warmth to the glorious life of the Trinity, the generous impulse that is the origin of the creation of man and the universe. All humanity is called to imitate this love of God, and every Christian vocation is a way of living out this sacred call. Religious life, single life, and married life are all integral pieces within the mosaic of Christianity's witness to the unbounded, unconditional love of God for his creation. In a particular way, the Sacrament of Marriage images the unity between Christ and his Church; as Pope John Paul II wrote: "One cannot understand the Church as the mystical body of Christ without reference to the 'great mystery,' linked to the creation of man as man and woman and to the vocation of both conjugal love, paternity and maternity."

Gianna Beretta Molla possessed the gift of knowing how to translate these ideals into loving action within her vocation to marriage: "There are many difficulties, but with the help of God we can go forward fearlessly, and if we should have to die struggling for our vocation, it would be the most beautiful day of our life." The collection of her letters to her husband allow us a precious glimpse into the wonders of love between spouses. In the joy of her engagement and first years of marriage, in the fullness of her years of maturity, when she opened herself to suffering, and in the tenderness of her last years, we see that marriage is a gift of grace, giving expression to the extraordinary love of God and making it visible. The letters show us Gianna's example and give us a more complete and profound interpretation of her life: the life of an ordinary woman dedicated to love.

A few days after Gianna's beatification, her sanctity was defined as "simple and accessible to everyone," not in the sense that it was effortless, but as a "message of grandeur" directed to all the faithful, particularly to women. Gianna's letters do not speak in a learned and inaccessible language, but they delineate a beautiful and delicate way, open to all.

BOOKS & MEDIA

The Daughters of St. Paul operate book and media centers at the following addresses. Visit, call or write the one nearest you today, or find us on the World Wide Web, www.pauline.org

CALIFORNIA
3908 Sepulveda Blvd, Culver City, CA 90230   310-397-8676
5945 Balboa Avenue, San Diego, CA 92111   858-565-9181
46 Geary Street, San Francisco, CA 94108   415-781-5180

FLORIDA
145 S.W. 107th Avenue, Miami, FL 33174   305-559-6715

HAWAII
1143 Bishop Street, Honolulu, HI 96813   808-521-2731
Neighbor Islands call: 800-259-8463

ILLINOIS
172 North Michigan Avenue, Chicago, IL 60601   312-346-4228

LOUISIANA
4403 Veterans Memorial Blvd, Metairie, LA 70006   504-887-7631

MASSACHUSETTS
Rte. 1, 885 Providence Hwy, Dedham, MA 02026   781-326-5385

MISSOURI
9804 Watson Road, St. Louis, MO 63126   314-965-3512

NEW JERSEY
561 U.S. Route 1, Wick Plaza, Edison, NJ 08817   732-572-1200

NEW YORK
150 East 52nd Street, New York, NY 10022   212-754-1110
78 Fort Place, Staten Island, NY 10301   718-447-5071

OHIO
2105 Ontario Street, Cleveland, OH 44115   216-621-9427

PENNSYLVANIA
9171-A Roosevelt Blvd, Philadelphia, PA 19114   215-676-9494

SOUTH CAROLINA
243 King Street, Charleston, SC 29401   843-577-0175

TENNESSEE
4811 Poplar Avenue, Memphis, TN 38117   901-761-2987

TEXAS
114 Main Plaza, San Antonio, TX 78205   210-224-8101

VIRGINIA
1025 King Street, Alexandria, VA 22314   703-549-3806

CANADA
3022 Dufferin Street, Toronto, Ontario, Canada M6B 3T5   416-781-9131
1155 Yonge Street, Toronto, Ontario, Canada M4T 1W2   416-934-3440

¡También somos su fuente para libros, videos y música en español!